The MAILBOX®
The Education Center®

Types of Writing

55 ready-to-use writing activities from the Writing Works!® series from The Mailbox® Books

- ○ **Narrative Writing**
- ○ **Persuasive Writing**
- ○ **Descriptive Writing**
- ○ **Expository Writing**

Plus additional prompts, assessment forms, and proofreading checklists!

Managing Editor: Debra Liverman

Editorial Team: Becky S. Andrews, Kimberley Bruck, Karen P. Shelton, Diane Badden, Cindy K. Daoust, Amy Payne, Karen A. Brudnak, Sarah Hamblet, Hope Rodgers, Dorothy C. McKinney

Production Team: Lisa K. Pitts, Pam Crane, Rebecca Saunders, Jennifer Tipton Cappoen, Chris Curry, Theresa Lewis Goode, Clint Moore, Greg D. Rieves, Barry Slate, Donna K. Teal, Zane Williard, Tazmen Carlisle, Irene Harvley-Felder, Amy Kirtley-Hill, Kristy Parton, Cathy Edwards Simrell, Lynette Dickerson, Mark Rainey

www.themailbox.com

©2005 The Mailbox®
All rights reserved.
ISBN10 #1-56234-664-4 • ISBN13 #978-156234-664-5

Manufactured in the United States
10 9 8 7 6 5 4 3 2

Table of Contents

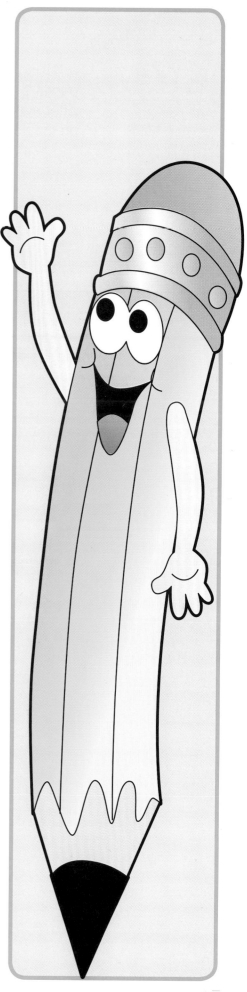

How to Use

Using *Types of Writing* is easy. Just turn to the table of contents on pages 2 and 3 to find a lesson on the type of writing you want to reinforce. After making student copies of the lesson's reproducible, follow the steps on the accompanying teacher page. It's that simple!

Each two-page lesson includes

Motivating writing prompt

Simple steps for the prewriting stage

Simple steps for the writing stage, including ideas for publishing or displaying students' work

Reproducible graphic organizer or pattern for final drafts

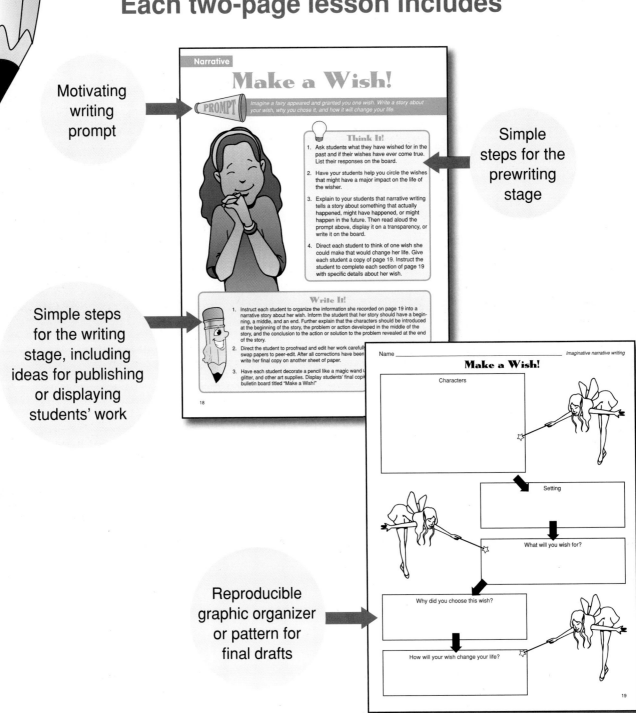

Look on pages 116–128 for these timesaving extras!

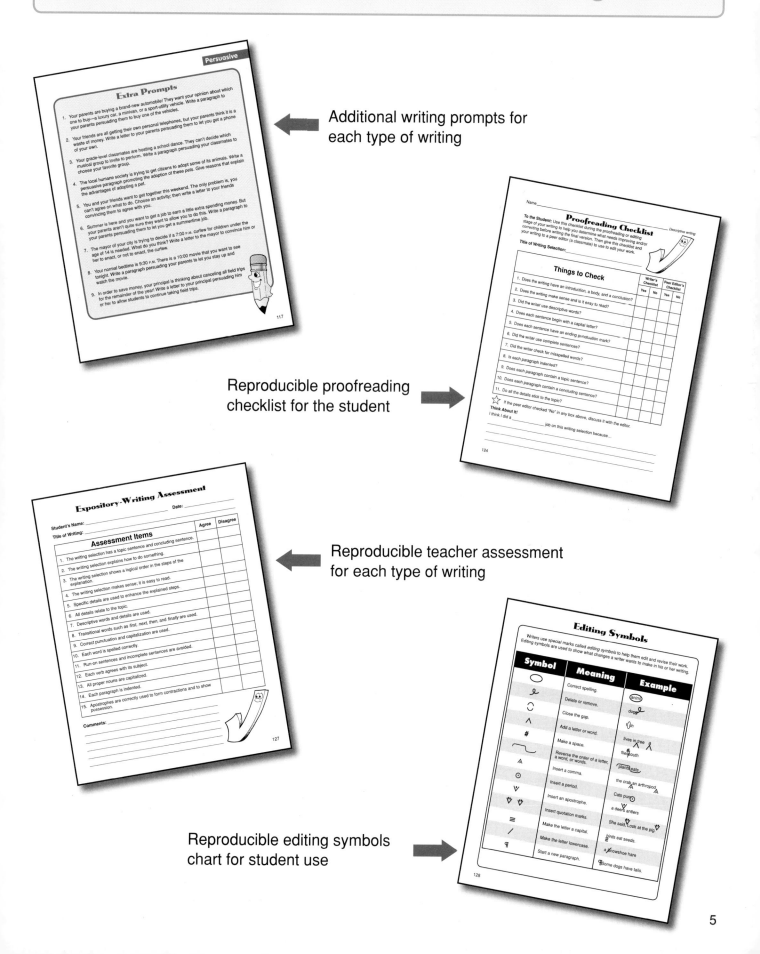

Additional writing prompts for each type of writing

Reproducible proofreading checklist for the student

Reproducible teacher assessment for each type of writing

Reproducible editing symbols chart for student use

And the Winner Is...

PROMPT *You've just won $100,000 in a contest! What will you do with the prize money? Write a story about what you plan to do with the $100,000.*

AMERICAN INSTANT
SUPER DUPER PRIZES

Check ___1___

$ 100,000

Pay to the order of Anne Salisbury

One hundred thousand dollars

William Cash
signature

AMERICAN
INSTANT
BANK, INC.

Think It!

1. Ask your students if any of them have ever entered a contest. Have student volunteers share the types of contests they've entered and if they became winners.

2. Explain to your students that narrative writing tells a story about something that actually happened, might have happened, or might happen in the future. Then read aloud the prompt above, display it on a transparency, or write it on the board.

3. Give each student a copy of page 7. Have the student complete each dollar bill on the reproducible by listing all the things she plans to do with the prize money.

Write It!

1. Have the student use another sheet of paper to write a story using the details she's listed on page 7. Inform the student that her story should have a beginning, a middle, and an end. Further explain that the characters should be introduced at the beginning of the story, the problem or action developed in the middle of the story, and the conclusion to the action or solution to the problem revealed at the end of the story.

2. Direct the student to proofread and edit her work carefully. Encourage students to swap papers to peer-edit. After all corrections have been made, have the student write her final copy on another sheet of paper and decorate the borders of the paper with dollar signs.

3. Allow each student to share her story. Then display the final copies on a bulletin board covered in green paper and titled "And the Winner Is…." Decorate the board with large dollar signs.

And the Winner Is...

Where would you go?

_____

_____

_____

What would you buy?

_____

_____

_____

With whom would you share the money?

_____

_____

_____

What would you do?

_____

_____

_____

Dear Diary,....

PROMPT *Imagine you're at Camp Sun and Fun for the summer. Write a diary entry about a typical day at camp.*

Think It!

1. Help students brainstorm a list of possible camp activities, such as making crafts, playing sports, and telling ghost stories. Write their responses on the board.

2. Explain to your students that narrative writing tells a story about something that actually happened, might have happened, or might happen in the future. Then read aloud the prompt above, display it on a transparency, or write it on the board.

3. Give each student a large sheet of drawing paper. Then instruct the student to draw four large circles on his sheet of paper.

4. Tell each student to select four camp activities listed on the board and then label the top of each circle with one of the selected activities. Next, direct the student to fill in each circle with three or four details related to each activity.

Write It!

1. Give each student a copy of page 9.

2. Instruct each student to use the reproducible as a guide in writing his story on another sheet of paper. Inform the student that his story should have a beginning, a middle, and an end. Further explain that the characters should be introduced at the beginning of the story, the problem or action developed in the middle of the story, and the conclusion to the action or solution to the problem revealed at the end of the story.

3. Direct the student to proofread and edit his work carefully. Encourage students to swap papers to peer-edit. After all corrections have been made, have the student write his final copy on page 9.

4. Have the student illustrate one activity from his day at camp on a sheet of drawing paper. Then compile each student's narrative and illustration in a class book titled "Dear Diary,…"

_____

(date)

Dear Diary,

   My day started when _____

_____

_____

_____

Next, _____

_____

_____

_____

Then, _____

_____

_____

_____

Finally, _____

_____

_____

_____

My Dream Vacation

PROMPT *Is there a special place you've always dreamed of visiting? Write a story about a dream vacation to this special place.*

Think It!

1. Tell students about a special vacation you have taken. Explain where you went, what you did, how long you stayed, and so on. Allow students time to discuss trips they have taken or would like to take.

2. Explain to your students that narrative writing tells a story about something that actually happened, might have happened, or might happen in the future. Read aloud the prompt above, display it on a transparency, or write it on the board.

3. Give each student a copy of page 11. Have the student fill in the suitcases on the reproducible with specific details related to each suitcase's topic.

Write It!

1. Direct each student to use details recorded on page 11 to help him write his story on another sheet of paper. Inform the student that his story should have a beginning, a middle, and an end. Further explain that the characters should be introduced at the beginning of the story, the problem or action developed in the middle of the story, and the conclusion to the activity or solution to the problem revealed at the end of the story.

2. Direct the student to proofread and edit his work carefully. Encourage students to swap papers to peer-edit. After all corrections have been made, have the student write his final copy on another sheet of paper.

3. Display students' final drafts on a bulletin board titled "Our Dream Vacations!" Decorate the board with travel brochures and magazine photographs of tourists, cameras, and vacation sites.

Name _____

My Dream Vacation

Who is going with you on your
vacation? _____
_____
_____
_____
_____

Where does your dream vacation
take place? _____
_____
_____
_____
_____

Event #1: _____
_____
_____
_____
_____
_____

Event #2: _____
_____
_____
_____
_____
_____

Event #3: _____
_____
_____
_____
_____
_____

Climax (The most exciting part of
your vacation): _____
_____
_____
_____
_____

How does your dream vacation end?
_____
_____
_____
_____
_____

Turn Back the Clock!

PROMPT *Have you ever wanted to be able to turn back the clock so you could change something you wish you had done differently? Write a story about a time you did something you wish you had done differently.*

Think It!

1. Tell students about a time you wish you had done something differently. Then explain how you would change the situation if you could turn back time.

2. Explain to your students that narrative writing tells a story about something that actually happened, might have happened, or might happen in the future. Then read aloud the prompt above, display it on a transparency, or write it on the board.

3. Give each student a copy of page 13 and instruct him to use the reproducible to record details about his story.

Write It!

1. Instruct each student to use the details (recorded on page 13) to help write his story. Inform the student that his story should have a beginning, a middle, and an end. Further explain that the characters should be introduced at the beginning of the story, the problem developed in the middle of the story, and the solution to the problem revealed at the end of the story.

2. Direct the student to proofread and edit his work carefully. Encourage students to swap papers to peer-edit. After all corrections have been made, have the student write his final copy on another sheet of paper.

3. Display the students' writings on a bulletin board titled "Turn Back the Clock!"

Turn Back the Clock!

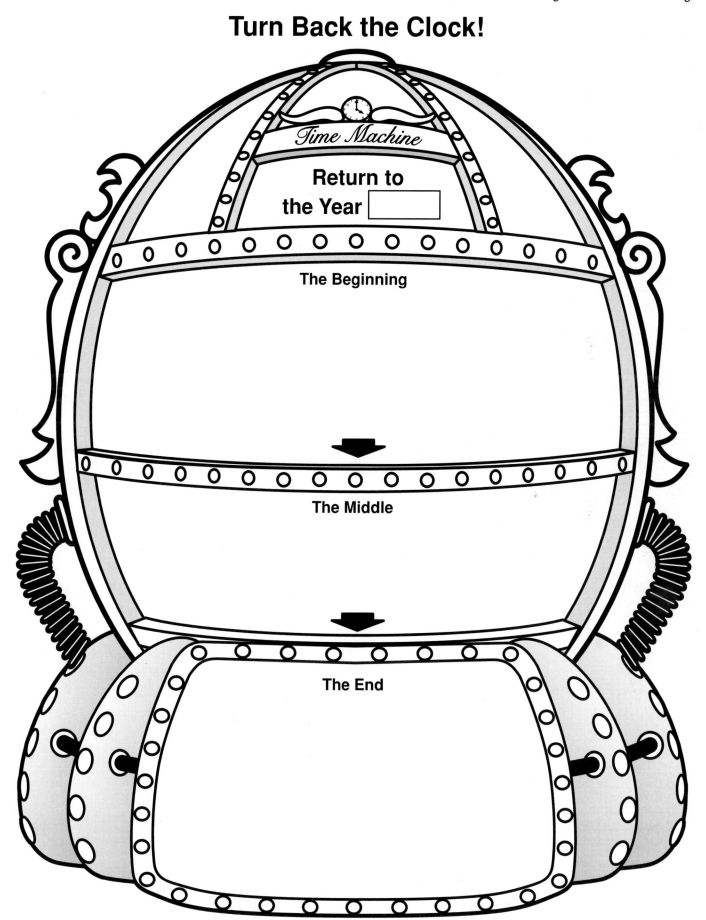

Time Machine

Return to the Year ☐

The Beginning

The Middle

The End

The Day I Met...

PROMPT *Imagine meeting your favorite sports star, movie star, or author. Write a story about meeting this person and how you'll spend the day together.*

Think It!

1. Ask students to think about someone famous they have always wanted to meet. List responses on the board in categories, such as "Sports Figures," "Actors," and "Singers."

2. Explain to your students that narrative writing tells a story about something that actually happened, might have happened, or might happen in the future. Then read aloud the prompt above, display it on a transparency, or write it on the board.

3. Discuss how each student might spend the day with this special person. For example, if her person is a sports star, she could attend the athlete's sporting event, or if her person is a singer, she could be a special guest at the performer's concert.

4. Give each student a copy of page 15 and direct her to use the reproducible to help plan a day with this special person.

Write It!

1. Direct each student to look over her plan from page 15 and circle the three most important things she wants to do with her special person.

2. Instruct each student to use another sheet of paper to write a story about her special day, including details of each event circled on page 15. Inform the student that her story should have a beginning, a middle, and an end. Further explain that the characters should be introduced at the beginning of the story, the problem or action developed in the middle of the story, and the conclusion to the activity or solution to the problem revealed at the end of the story.

3. Direct the student to proofread and edit her work carefully. Encourage students to swap papers to peer-edit. After all corrections have been made, have the student write her final copy on another sheet of paper.

4. Give each student a sheet of drawing paper. Instruct the student to draw a picture of herself with her special person. Compile students' illustrations and narratives into a class book titled "The Day I Met...." Have each student sign her name on the author's page. Display the book in your school's library for other classes to enjoy!

_____'s **Day Planner**
(student's name)

Date: _____

My Special Person: _____

Our Schedule:

8:00 A.M. _____

_____

9:00 A.M. _____

_____

10:00 A.M. _____

_____

11:00 A.M. _____

_____

12:00 P.M. _____

_____

1:00 P.M. _____

_____

2:00 P.M. _____

_____

3:00 P.M. _____

_____

4:00 P.M. _____

_____

5:00 P.M. _____

_____

6:00 P.M. _____

_____

7:00 P.M. _____

_____

8:00 P.M. *Say goodbye to my special friend.*

_____

If I Were President...

PROMPT *The president works hard to make our country a better place in which to live and work. Imagine you are running for president. Write a story about running for the office of president.*

Nice to meet you, Ms. President

Think It!

1. With your class, brainstorm ways the president tries to make our country better, such as boosting the economy and enforcing laws. List students' responses on the board.

2. Explain to your students that narrative writing tells a story about something that actually happened, might have happened, or might happen in the future. Then read aloud the prompt above, display it on a transparency, or write it on the board.

3. Give each student a copy of page 17. Instruct the student to use the reproducible to help her organize her thoughts and ideas for her story.

Write It!

1. Direct the student to use the ideas recorded on page 17 to help her write the story on another sheet of paper. Inform the student that her story should have a beginning, a middle, and an end. Further explain that the characters should be introduced at the beginning of the story, the problem or action developed in the middle of the story, and the conclusion to the activity or solution to the problem revealed at the end of the story.

2. Direct the student to proofread and edit her work carefully. Encourage students to swap papers to peer-edit. Have the student write her final version on a sheet of notebook paper and trim the edges of the paper to resemble a speech bubble.

3. Give each student a sheet of drawing paper on which to draw a self-portrait of herself giving a speech. Or take a Polaroid of the student acting out this role. Display each illustration (or photograph) next to its corresponding speech bubble on a bulletin board titled "If I Were President...."

Imaginative narrative writing

If I Were President...

The Beginning
(Characters and Setting)

The Middle
(Problem or Action)

The End
(Conclusion or Solution)

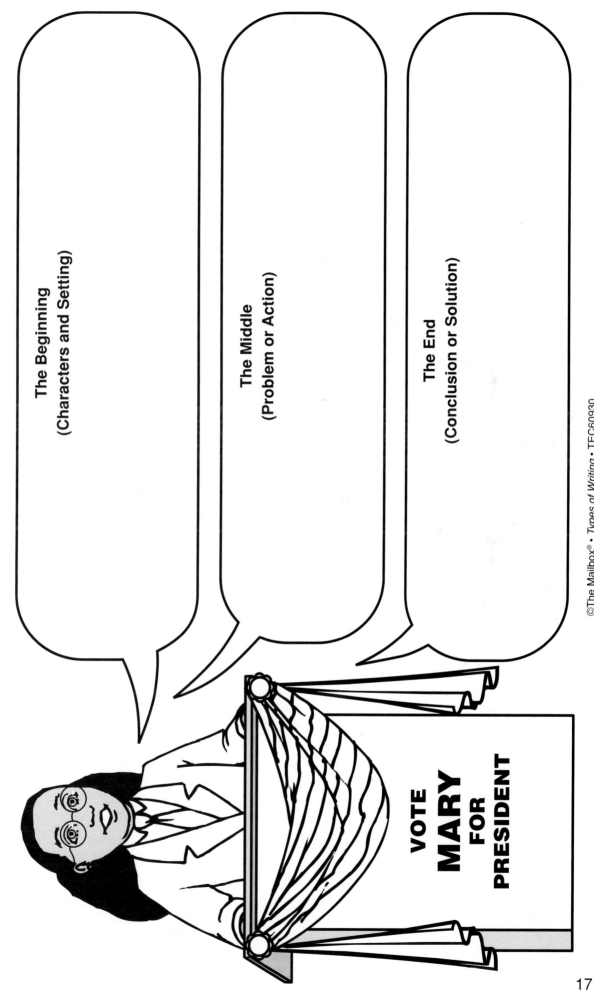

VOTE
MARY
FOR
PRESIDENT

Make a Wish!

PROMPT
Imagine a fairy appeared and granted you one wish. Write a story about your wish, why you chose it, and how it will change your life.

Think It!

1. Ask students what they have wished for in the past and if their wishes have ever come true. List their responses on the board.

2. Have your students help you circle the wishes that might have a major impact on the life of the wisher.

3. Explain to your students that narrative writing tells a story about something that actually happened, might have happened, or might happen in the future. Then read aloud the prompt above, display it on a transparency, or write it on the board.

4. Direct each student to think of one wish she could make that would change her life. Give each student a copy of page 19. Instruct the student to complete each section of page 19 with specific details about her wish.

Write It!

1. Instruct each student to organize the information she recorded on page 19 into a narrative story about her wish. Inform the student that her story should have a beginning, a middle, and an end. Further explain that the characters should be introduced at the beginning of the story, the problem or action developed in the middle of the story, and the conclusion to the action or solution to the problem revealed at the end of the story.

2. Direct the student to proofread and edit her work carefully. Encourage students to swap papers to peer-edit. After all corrections have been made, have the student write her final copy on another sheet of paper.

3. Have each student decorate a pencil like a magic wand using scraps of material, glitter, and other art supplies. Display students' final copies and magic wands on a bulletin board titled "Make a Wish!"

Make a Wish!

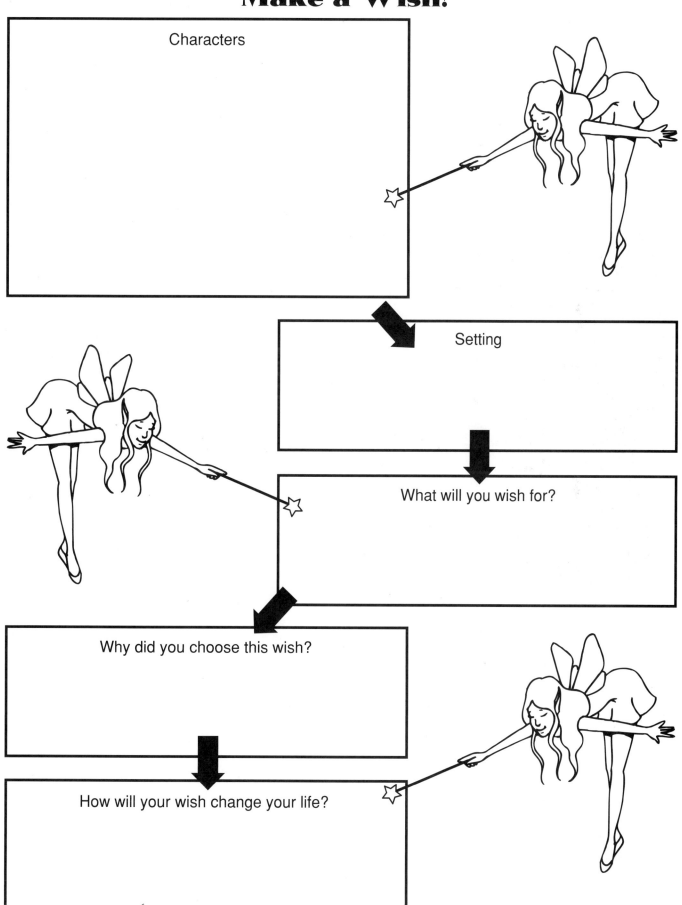

Characters

Setting

What will you wish for?

Why did you choose this wish?

How will your wish change your life?

The Perfect Pet

PROMPT *If you could have any pet, what would it be? Write a story about searching for and finding the perfect pet.*

Think It!

1. Discuss with students how having a pet can be like having a friend. Further explain that pets make great company and they're fun to be around and fun to play with. Then help your students brainstorm a list of possible pets. Record their responses on the board.

2. Explain to your students that narrative writing tells a story about something that actually happened, might have happened, or might happen in the future. Then read aloud the prompt above, display it on a transparency, or write it on the board.

3. Give each student a copy of page 21 and direct her to use the reproducible to help her plan a story about obtaining the perfect pet.

Write It!

1. Instruct the student to use the details (recorded on page 21) to help write her story. Inform the student that her story should have a beginning, a middle, and an end. Further explain that the characters should be introduced at the beginning of the story, the problem or action developed in the middle of the story, and the conclusion to the activity or solution to the problem revealed at the end of the story.

2. Direct the student to proofread and edit her work carefully. Encourage students to swap papers to peer-edit. After all corrections have been made, have the student write her final copy on another sheet of paper.

3. Give each student a large sheet of tagboard and a pair of scissors. Have the student cut the tagboard into the shape of her perfect pet, a doghouse, a pet-food bowl, or any shape related to her pet. Remind the student to make the cutout large enough to hold the final copy of her story. Then instruct the student to glue her final copy onto the center of the cutout.

4. Display the completed writings and cutouts on a wall or bulletin board titled "Perfect Pets."

Name ____________________ *Imaginative narrative writing*

The Perfect Pet

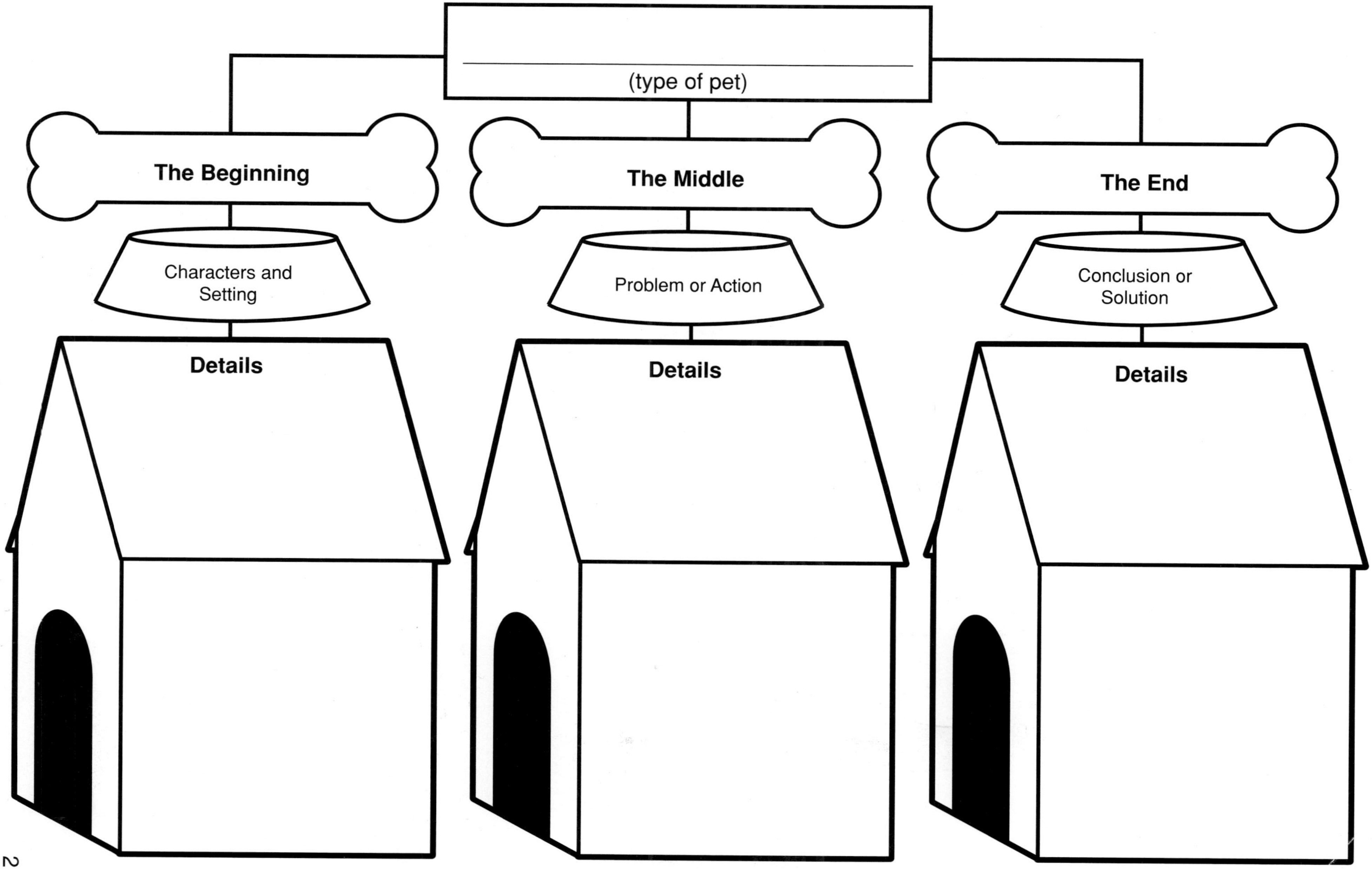

(type of pet)
The Beginning
Characters and Setting
Details
The Middle
Problem or Action
Details
The End
Conclusion or Solution
Details

The Championship Game

PROMPT *After school many students play sports for fun. Write a story about winning the championship game of your favorite sport.*

Think It!

1. Help students brainstorm various after-school sports. List their responses on the board.

2. Explain to your students that narrative writing tells a story about something that actually happened, might have happened, or might happen in the future. Then read aloud the prompt above, display it on a transparency, or write it on the board.

3. Instruct each student to choose one sport listed on the board as her writing topic.

4. Give each student a copy of page 23 and have her fill in the boxes with details about her chosen sport.

Write It!

1. Have each student use the information recorded on page 23 to write her story on another sheet of paper. Inform the student that her story should have a beginning, a middle, and an end. Further explain that the characters should be introduced at the beginning of the story, the problem or action developed in the middle of the story, and the conclusion to the activity or solution to the problem revealed at the end of the story.

2. Direct the student to proofread and edit her work carefully. Encourage students to swap papers to peer-edit. After all corrections have been made, have the student write her final copy on another sheet of paper.

3. Give each student a large sheet of construction paper and instruct her to cut out the shape of an object related to her sport such as a large football, baseball glove, or helmet.

4. Instruct each student to glue her final writing to the center of the cutout shape. Display students' final copies around the room or on a bulletin board titled "The Championship Game."

The Championship Game

_____

(Name of sport)

Other people involved in this sport:

_____

_____

_____

The beginning of the game:

_____

_____

_____

_____

_____

_____

Problems that occurred:

_____

_____

_____

_____

_____

_____

_____

_____

Accomplishments / Great plays:

_____

_____

_____

_____

_____

_____

The end of the game:

_____

_____

_____

Dream Jobs!

PROMPT *Imagine yourself 15 to 20 years from now in a career, such as teaching, fire fighting, or scientific research. Write a story about your first day on the job of your future career.*

Think It!

1. Discuss your profession with students, why you chose it, and what it is like. Let students share their dream jobs with the class as you record them on the board or overhead projector.

2. Explain to your students that narrative writing tells a story about something that actually happened, might have happened, or might happen in the future. Then read aloud the prompt above, display it on a transparency, or write it on the board.

3. Give each student a copy of page 25. In the cloud labeled "Who..." on page 25, instruct each student to list all the characters involved in her story. In the "Where..." cloud, have the student list details about the type of place in which she sees herself working, such as an office building, a post office, or the outdoors. In the "What..." cloud, have her list details about what happens during her first day on the job.

Write It!

1. Instruct each student to use the information she recorded on page 25 to help her write on another sheet of paper a story about her first day. Inform the student that her story should have a beginning, a middle, and an end. Further explain that the characters should be introduced at the beginning of the story, the problem or action developed in the middle of the story, and the conclusion to the activity or solution to the problem revealed at the end of the story.

2. Direct the student to proofread and edit her work carefully. Encourage students to swap papers to peer-edit. After all corrections have been made, have each student write her final copy on another sheet of paper.

3. Give each student a sheet of blue construction paper and a piece of white chalk. Instruct the student to paste her final writing to the center of the construction paper. Then have her use the chalk to draw clouds on the construction paper border around her writing.

4. Display students' work on a bulletin board titled "Our Dream Jobs!"

My Dream Job!

Who are the characters in your story?

Where will you work?

What will you do on your first day?

Turning Points

When people have experiences that change their lives, they call those experiences turning points. Write a story about an event that has been a turning point in your life and explain how you changed.

Think It!

1. Discuss with students a personal turning point in your life. It might be a marriage, the birth of a child, a move, etc. Don't forget to describe how you felt. Then have students share some of their own turning points. Events such as hitting a home run, changing schools, or making a new friend can be milestones in a young person's life. Record their responses on the board.

2. Explain to your students that narrative writing tells a story about something that actually happened, might have happened, or might happen in the future. Then read aloud the prompt above, display it on a transparency, or write it on the board.

3. Give each student a copy of page 27. Direct him to use the reproducible to help gather and organize his thoughts.

Write It!

1. Have each student use the information recorded on page 27 to help write, on another sheet of paper, a journal entry about his turning point. Remind students to use words that describe how that change felt by including dialogue, setting, sequence of events, and other details.

2. Encourage students to swap papers for peer response. After all changes have been made, direct each student to write the final version of his journal entry on another sheet of paper.

3. For proper display, have each student follow these directions: (a) turn your page so that the writing is upside down, but faceup, (b) turn your page over as if you're turning the page of a book, and (c) illustrate your journal entry. Display the finished projects on a bulletin board with the pictures facing out and attached only at the top. When students see a picture that they want to learn more about, all they need to do is lift the picture to read the student's journal entry. Title the display "Turning Points."

Turning Points

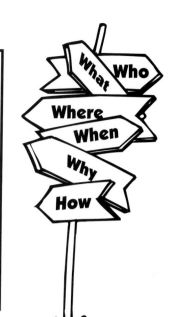

Who: _____

What: _____

Where: _____

When: _____

Why: _____

How: _____

Topic Sentence:

_____

_____

_____

_____

Your Feelings:
(Use sensory words and specific details.)

_____

_____

_____

_____

_____

_____

_____

_____

_____

_____

_____

Conclusion:
(The significance of this event in your life)

_____

_____

_____

_____

_____

_____

Definitely Different Days!

PROMPT

Have you ever had a day that was really different from your usual daily routine? Write a story about such a day and what made it so unique.

Think It!

1. Describe for students a typical day in your life. Then tell about a day that was full of surprises or unusual events. Ask several student volunteers to share unusual or different days they have experienced.

2. Explain to your students that narrative writing tells a story about something that actually happened, might have happened, or might happen in the future. Then read aloud the prompt above, display it on a transparency, or write it on the board.

3. Give each student a copy of page 29. Have the student use this reproducible to organize his thoughts about his unique day.

Write It!

1. Have each student use another sheet of paper to write a five-paragraph narrative story about his unique day. Inform the student that his story should have a beginning, a middle, and an end. Further explain that the characters should be introduced at the beginning of the story, the problem or action developed in the middle of the story, and the conclusion to the activity or solution to the problem revealed at the end of the story.

2. Direct the student to proofread and edit his work carefully. Encourage students to swap papers to peer-edit. After all corrections have been made, instruct the student to write his final copy on another sheet of paper.

3. If desired, create a bulletin board display that resembles a giant monthly calendar. Display each student's final writing in a separate block or day on the calendar. Title the display "Definitely Different Days!"

My Definitely Different Day!

What did you do **first** on your different day?	What did you do **next?**	**Then** what happened?	What happened **after** that?	How did your different day **end?**

A Special Gift

 *It's nice to receive gifts, but sometimes it feels even better to give them. Write a story about a time you gave someone a special gift.*

Think It!

1. Prior to beginning this writing activity, ask each student to bring in wrapping paper, a bow, and an empty box, such as a shirt or shoe box.

2. Discuss with your students different gifts they have been given and how they felt receiving them. Then discuss times they felt happy about giving gifts.

3. Explain to your students that narrative writing tells a story about something that actually happened, might have happened, or might happen in the future. Then read aloud the prompt above, display it on a transparency, or write it on the board.

4. Give each student a copy of page 31 and direct him to fill in each section of the present with specific details about a special gift he has given someone.

Write It!

1. Direct the student to use the details he has listed on the front of page 31 to help him write his story on another sheet of paper. Inform the student that his story should have a beginning, a middle, and an end. Further explain that the characters should be introduced at the beginning of the story, the problem or action developed in the middle of the story, and the conclusion to the activity or solution to the problem revealed at the end of the story.

2. Direct the student to proofread and edit his work carefully. Encourage students to swap papers to peer-edit. After all corrections have been made, have the student write his final copy on another sheet of paper.

3. Instruct each student to cover his gift box with wrapping paper, then top it with a bow. Then have the student attach the final version of his story to the front of his gift box. Display the boxes under the title "Our Special Gifts."

A Special Gift

Beginning:

Whom was the gift for? _____

_____

_____

_____

Middle:

Why did you give the gift, and what type of gift did you

give? _____

_____

_____

_____

Middle:

How did the person react upon receiving the gift? _____

_____

_____

_____

End:

How did giving the gift make you feel? _____

_____

_____

_____

©The Mailbox® • *Types of Writing* • TEC60930

31

My Special Treasure

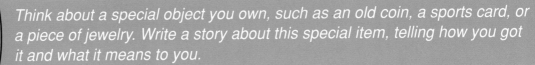

PROMPT *Think about a special object you own, such as an old coin, a sports card, or a piece of jewelry. Write a story about this special item, telling how you got it and what it means to you.*

Think It!

1. Tell your students about something you own that has special meaning. If possible, bring in the item to show your students. Ask students about some of the special objects they own. List these on the board.

2. Explain to your students that narrative writing tells a story about something that actually happened, might have happened, or might happen in the future. Then read aloud the prompt above, display it on a transparency, or write it on the board.

3. Give each student a copy of page 33. Then instruct the student to use the reproducible to help him organize his thoughts about his story's beginning, middle, and end.

Write It!

1. Instruct each student to use the information (recorded on page 33) to help him write the story. Remind the student that his story should have a beginning, a middle, and an end. Further explain that the characters should be introduced at the beginning of the story, the problem or action developed in the middle of the story, and the conclusion of the activity or solution to the problem revealed at the end of the story.

2. Direct the student to proofread and edit his work carefully. Encourage students to swap papers to peer-edit. After all corrections have been made, have the student write his final copy on another sheet of paper.

3. Give each student a pair of scissors and a large sheet of construction paper. Instruct him to draw and cut out a treasure chest pattern large enough to hold his final draft. Then direct the student to paste his final draft onto the center of the cutout.

4. Display students' final drafts on a bulletin board titled "Our Treasures!" As a finishing touch, staple gold construction paper coins around the border of the board.

Name ______________________________ *Personal narrative writing*

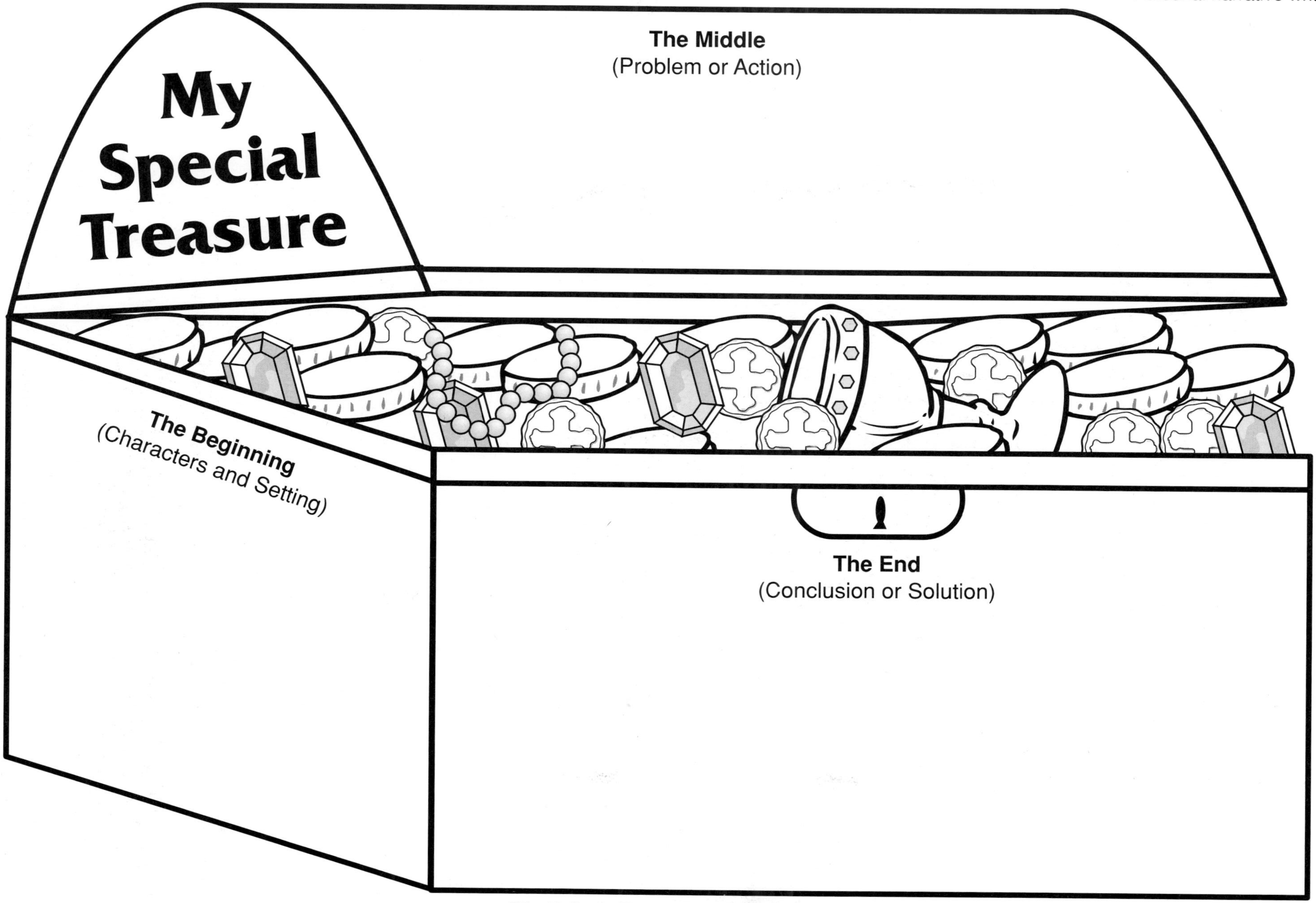

My Special Treasure
The Middle
(Problem or Action)
The Beginning
(Characters and Setting)
The End
(Conclusion or Solution)

Change Is in the Air

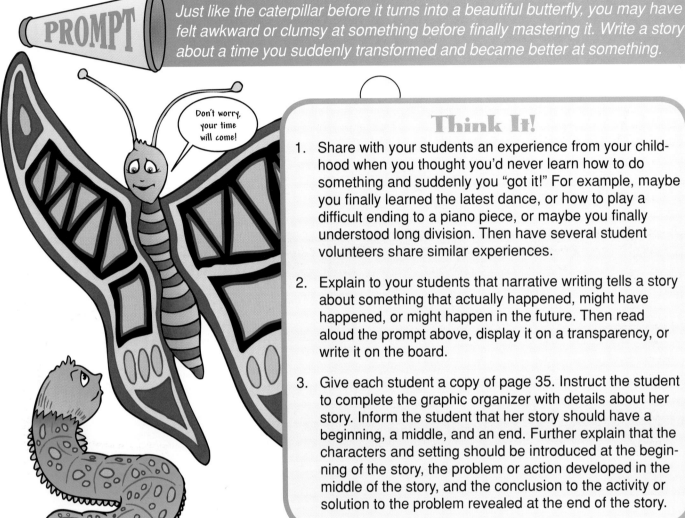

PROMPT *Just like the caterpillar before it turns into a beautiful butterfly, you may have felt awkward or clumsy at something before finally mastering it. Write a story about a time you suddenly transformed and became better at something.*

Don't worry, your time will come!

Think It!

1. Share with your students an experience from your childhood when you thought you'd never learn how to do something and suddenly you "got it!" For example, maybe you finally learned the latest dance, or how to play a difficult ending to a piano piece, or maybe you finally understood long division. Then have several student volunteers share similar experiences.

2. Explain to your students that narrative writing tells a story about something that actually happened, might have happened, or might happen in the future. Then read aloud the prompt above, display it on a transparency, or write it on the board.

3. Give each student a copy of page 35. Instruct the student to complete the graphic organizer with details about her story. Inform the student that her story should have a beginning, a middle, and an end. Further explain that the characters and setting should be introduced at the beginning of the story, the problem or action developed in the middle of the story, and the conclusion to the activity or solution to the problem revealed at the end of the story.

Write It!

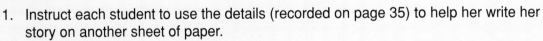

1. Instruct each student to use the details (recorded on page 35) to help her write her story on another sheet of paper.

2. Direct the student to proofread and edit her work carefully. Encourage students to swap papers to peer-edit. After all corrections have been made, have the student write her final copy on another sheet of paper.

3. Give each student a large sheet of tagboard, markers or crayons, glue, and scissors. Instruct each student to draw a large butterfly pattern on the tagboard. Then have the student cut out the pattern and glue her final writing onto the center of the pattern. Next, direct the student to decorate both sides of the butterfly with vibrant colorful patterns.

4. Punch a hole in the tops of the butterfly patterns and use lengths of string to hang them from the ceiling of your classroom. Or, display the butterflies on a bulletin board titled "Change Is in the Air."

Name _____

Change Is in the Air

The End
(Conclusion or Solution)

The Middle
(Problem or Action)

The Beginning
(Characters and Setting)

Let's Celebrate!

PROMPT

Whether it's for a special occasion, a holiday, or a party at a friend's house, everyone enjoys a good celebration. Write a story telling about a memorable celebration.

Think It!

1. Discuss with students the reasons for a celebration, and list their responses on the board. (Examples might include marriages, the birth of a baby, birthdays, and holidays.)

2. Explain to your students that narrative writing tells a story about something that actually happened, might have happened, or might happen in the future. Then read aloud the prompt above, display it on a transparency, or write it on the board.

3. Give each student a copy of page 37. Instruct the student to complete each balloon on the reproducible with details about his story.

Write It!

1. Instruct each student to use the details (recorded on page 37) to write his celebration story. Inform the student that his story should have a beginning, a middle, and an end. Further explain that the characters should be introduced at the beginning of the story, the problem or action developed in the middle of the story, and the conclusion to the activity or solution to the problem revealed at the end of the story.

2. Direct the student to proofread and edit his work carefully. Encourage students to swap papers to peer-edit. After all corrections have been made, have the student write his final copy on another sheet of paper.

3. If desired, use the following idea to display your students' writings. Give each student a large sheet of brightly colored construction paper. Have the student paste his final writing onto the center of the construction paper. Next, direct him to cut the construction paper around the writing into the shape of a balloon.

4. Attach a length of string to the bottom of each balloon. Then display the balloons on a wall or bulletin board titled "Let's Celebrate!" Decorate the area around the display with party hats, streamers, noisemakers, and other party favors.

Let's Celebrate!

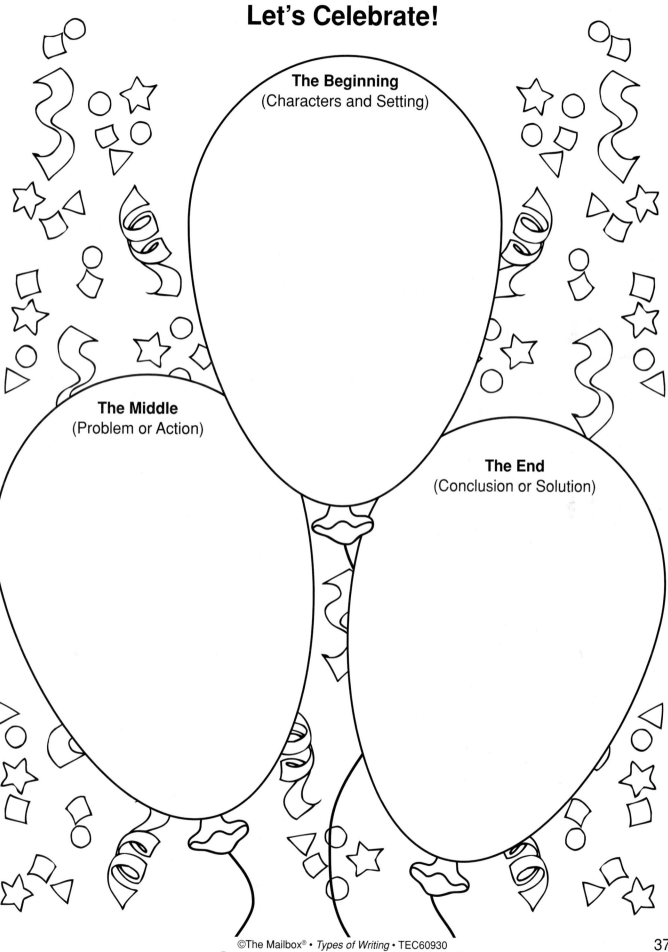

The Beginning
(Characters and Setting)

The Middle
(Problem or Action)

The End
(Conclusion or Solution)

My Favorite Time of the Year

PROMPT *Winter, spring, summer, or fall—which is your favorite time of the year? Write a story about something that happened during your favorite season.*

Think It!

1. Ask students to name the four seasons. Then write them at the top of the board. For each season, brainstorm with students different activities they can do during that time of year and then write each activity under its corresponding heading.

2. Explain to your students that narrative writing tells a story about something that actually happened, might have happened, or might happen in the future. Then read aloud the prompt above, display it on a transparency, or write it on the board.

3. Give each student a copy of page 39 and direct her to list details about her story for each section of the reproducible.

Write It!

1. Instruct each student to use the details (recorded on page 39) to help her write her story. Inform the student that her story should have a beginning, a middle, and an end. Further explain that the characters should be introduced at the beginning of the story, the problem or action developed in the middle of the story, and the conclusion to the activity or solution to the problem revealed at the end of the story.

2. Direct the student to proofread and edit her work carefully. Encourage students to swap papers to peer-edit. After all corrections have been made, have the student write her final copy on another sheet of paper.

3. If desired, use the following idea to display your students' final drafts. Divide a bulletin board into four equal sections. Label each section with the name of a different season.

4. Post each student's writing in the appropriate section of the bulletin board. Decorate the remaining space in each section with paper cutouts related to each season, such as leaves, snowflakes, suns, flowers, etc. Title the display "Reasons for Our Seasons!"

My Favorite Time of the Year

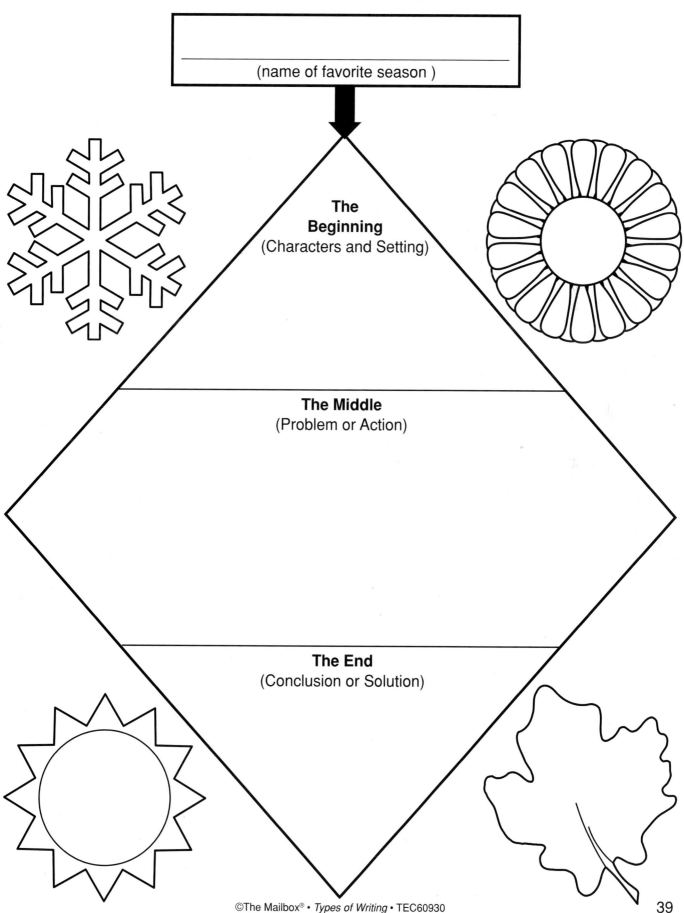

_____

(name of favorite season)

**The
Beginning**
(Characters and Setting)

The Middle
(Problem or Action)

The End
(Conclusion or Solution)

Best Friends

PROMPT *Think about someone you consider to be a best friend. Write a story about a time this friend helped you out or stood up for you.*

Think It!

1. Brainstorm with students the qualities that make a person a best friend. Record students' responses on the board or overhead. Then choose a few student volunteers and have each one share an experience when a best friend helped him out or stood up for him.

2. Explain to your students that narrative writing tells a story about something that actually happened, might have happened, or might happen in the future. Then read aloud the prompt above, display it on a transparency, or write it on the board.

3. Give each student a copy of page 41. Instruct the student to use the reproducible to help him organize his thoughts and ideas for his story.

Write It!

1. Direct the student to use the ideas recorded on page 41 to help him write the story on another sheet of paper. Inform the student that his story should have a beginning, a middle, and an end. Further explain that the characters should be introduced at the beginning of the story, the problem or action developed in the middle of the story, and the conclusion to the activity or solution to the problem revealed at the end of the story.

2. Have the student proofread and edit his work carefully. Encourage students to swap papers to peer-edit. After all corrections have been made, have the student write his final copy on another sheet of paper.

3. Give each student a large sheet of lightly colored construction paper. Instruct the student to paste his final writing on one side of the construction paper, then draw a picture of his best friend on the other side. Use a length of string to hang each student's work from the ceiling.

Name _____

Best Friend Story Map

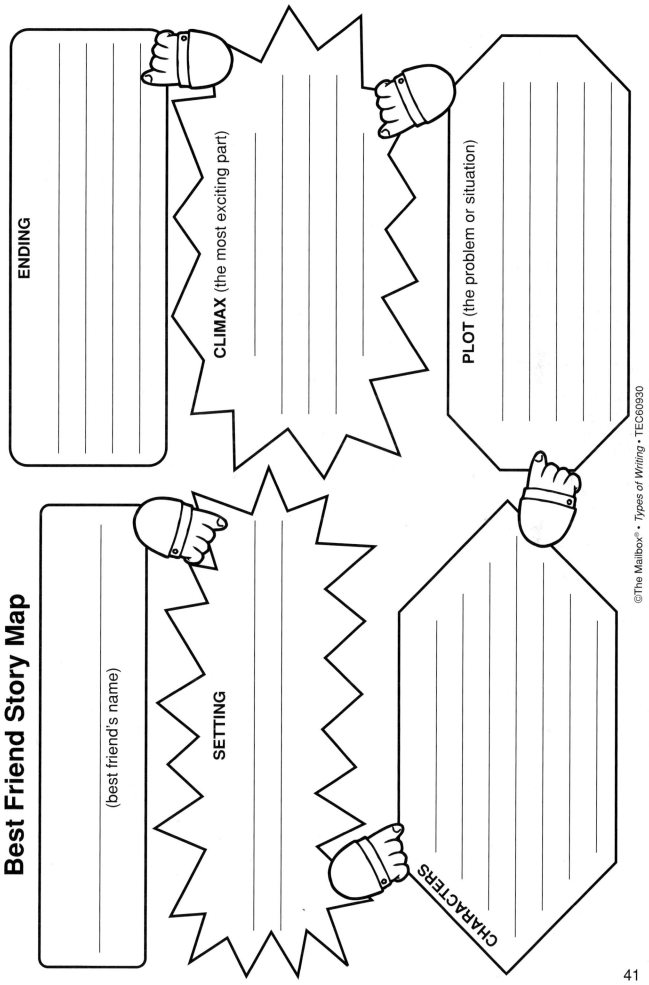

ENDING

CLIMAX (the most exciting part)

PLOT (the problem or situation)

(best friend's name)

SETTING

CHARACTERS

Rules Are Rules!

PROMPT *Rules are meant to keep things orderly and to keep people safe. Write about a time you broke a rule and the consequences you experienced.*

Think It!

1. Discuss with students why we have rules. Mention that rules keep us safe, and they provide guidelines for things we can and cannot do. Have your students help you list on the board some of your classroom or school rules.

2. Explain to your students that narrative writing tells a story about something that actually happened, might have happened, or might happen in the future. Then read aloud the prompt above, display it on a transparency, or write it on the board.

3. Give each student a copy of page 43. Instruct each student to use the reproducible to help him organize his thoughts about the story.

Write It!

1. Direct each student to use the details (recorded on page 43) to help him begin writing the rough draft of his story on another sheet of paper. Inform the student that his story should have a beginning, a middle, and an end. Further explain that the characters should be introduced at the beginning of the story, the problem or action developed in the middle of the story, and the conclusion to the activity or solution to the problem revealed at the end of the story.

2. Direct the student to proofread and edit his work carefully. Encourage students to swap papers to peer-edit. After all corrections have been made, have the student write his final copy on another sheet of paper.

3. Have the student choose the shape of one road sign, such as a yield or a stop sign. Next, give him a large sheet of construction paper in the color appropriate for his sign. Instruct the student to cut out the shape of his chosen sign, making sure the cutout is large enough to hold his final copy. Then have the student paste his final writing onto the center of the cutout.

4. Have each student share his writing with the rest of the class. Then display students' signs on a bulletin board titled "Rules Are Rules!"

Name _____

Rules Are Rules!

The End

What were the consequences of breaking this rule? How does your story end?

Details

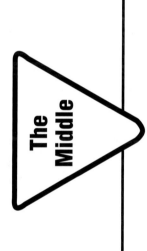

The Middle

What rule did you break, why did you break it, and what problems did it cause?

Details

The Beginning

What characters are in your story and where does it take place?

Details

My Life's Highway

PROMPT *Take a trip down the highway of your life. Think about the people you have met and experiences that you have had along the way. Write a story about one of your most vivid memories.*

Think It!

1. Have students brainstorm life experiences. Encourage them to share details about family members, friends, favorite things, important school events, special abilities, and hobbies and interests.

2. Explain to your students that narrative writing tells a story about something that actually happened, might have happened, or might happen in the future. Then read aloud the prompt above, display it on a transparency, or write it on the board.

3. Give each student a copy of page 45 and have him use the reproducible to write notes about his life experiences and his dreams for the future. Encourage him to use sensory details and emotions related to his experiences.

Write It!

1. Instruct each student to use the details (recorded on page 45) to help him write a story. Encourage him to use specific and accurate details about his life experiences.

2. Have students swap papers for peer response. After all changes have been made, direct the student to write the final version of his memoir on a 5" x 8" sheet of paper.

3. Have students make license plates by cutting 6" x 9" tagboard rectangles. Allow time for them to illustrate their license plates with decorative borders. Glue the memoirs to the center of the plates. Enlarge the road signs and pictures shown on page 45 and have students color them. Create a bulletin board titled "Driving Life's Highway" with a drawing of a road, the road signs, and pictures. Display the license plate stories for everyone to enjoy.

My Life's Highway

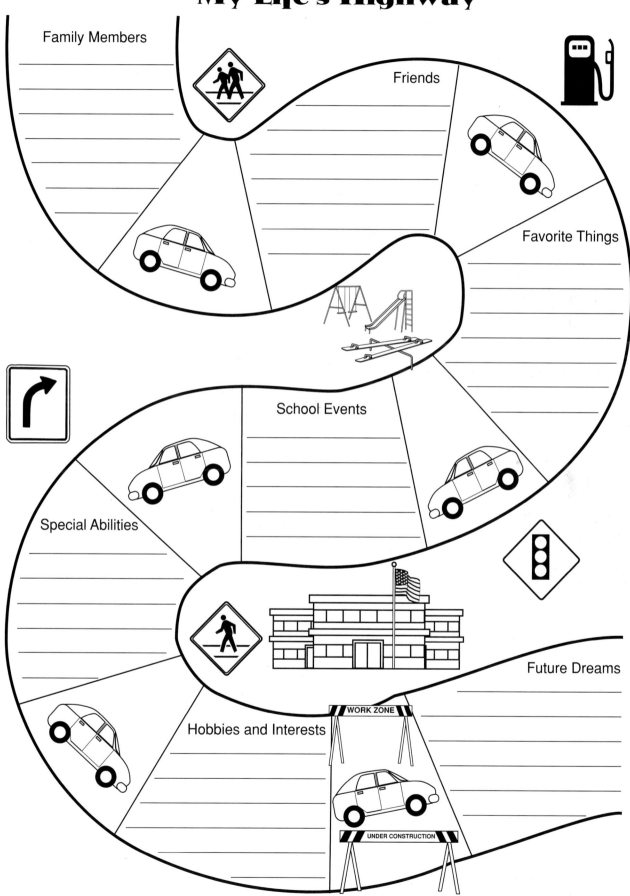

Family Members

Friends

Favorite Things

School Events

Special Abilities

Hobbies and Interests

Future Dreams

WORK ZONE

UNDER CONSTRUCTION

Go, Mascot!

PROMPT *Your school is selecting a new mascot. The selection committee wants to choose a mascot that will best represent your school. Write a letter persuading the committee that your mascot choice is the best one.*

Think It!

1. Have students name the mascots of their favorite sports teams. Record their responses on the board. Challenge them to explain why each organization may have chosen its particular mascot.

2. Tell students what your favorite team is and what its mascot is. Give reasons why the mascot is an appropriate choice, using facts and opinions. Point out to students that when attempting to convince someone of something, it is important to state facts to support your opinion.

3. Explain to students that when writing to persuade someone, the writer tries to convince the reader(s) that her opinion is the best one. She states her opinion at the beginning; gives details or reasons that prove, explain, or support it; and concludes by restating her opinion.

4. Read aloud the prompt above, display it on a transparency, or write it on the board.

5. Give each student a copy of page 47. Have the student use the reproducible to organize her thoughts and ideas.

Write It!

1. Instruct the student to use the information recorded on page 47 to help write a letter persuading the selection committee that her choice for the school mascot is the best one. Have her write her letter on another sheet of paper. Remind the student to include a topic sentence, at least three strong supporting details, and a concluding sentence.

2. Direct the student to proofread and edit her work carefully. Encourage students to swap papers to peer-edit. After all corrections have been made, have the student write her final copy on a sheet of paper.

3. If desired, give each student a pennant cut out of light-colored construction paper. Have the student draw and color a picture of the new mascot on the pennant. Then display the pennants, along with the completed letters, where others can enjoy them.

Go, Mascot!

**Opinion/
Topic Sentence:** _____

_____

**Supporting
Details:**

1. _____

_____

_____

_____

2. _____

_____

_____

3. _____

_____

_____

4. _____

_____

_____

5. _____

_____

_____

Conclusion: _____

_____

Road to Recycling

PROMPT *Reduce, reuse, recycle! Your community has started a recycling program, but many people aren't participating. Write a paragraph persuading people to recycle.*

Think It!

1. Pair students and have each pair list five classroom and five household objects that could be recycled.

2. As a class, brainstorm reasons why people should recycle. Record student responses on the board, having students identify each factual reason. Point out to students that when attempting to convince someone of something, it is important to state facts to support your opinion.

3. Explain to students that when writing to persuade, the writer tries to convince the reader(s) that his opinion is the best one. He states his opinion at the beginning; gives details or reasons that prove, explain, or support it; and concludes by restating his opinion.

4. Read aloud the prompt above, display it on a transparency, or write it on the board.

5. Give each student a copy of page 49. Have him use the reproducible to organize his thoughts and ideas about why people should recycle.

Write It!

1. Instruct each student to use the information recorded on page 49 to help write his paragraph. Remind the student to include a topic sentence, at least three strong supporting details, and a concluding sentence.

2. Direct the student to proofread and edit his work carefully. Encourage students to swap papers to peer-edit. After all corrections have been made, have each student write his final copy in the space provided on page 49.

3. If desired, have each student cut out the pattern along the bold lines and then color it and fold it along the thin lines to create a brochure. Lend the brochures to a younger class so they too can learn about the importance of recycling.

Name _____

Road to Recycling

Get on the Road to Recycling!

RECYCLE!

Opinion/Topic Sentence:

_____
_____

Reasons:

1 _____

2 _____

3 _____

4 _____

5 _____

Conclusion:

_____

©The Mailbox® • Types of Writing • TEC60930

Final Copy:

_____
_____
_____
_____
_____
_____
_____
_____
_____
_____
_____

Let's Eat!

PROMPT *You've been hired by your favorite fast-food restaurant to help write an advertisement promoting it. Write a paragraph persuading people that this restaurant is the best place to eat.*

Think It!

1. As a class, brainstorm a list of fast-food restaurants. Have volunteers name reasons why each restaurant is appealing, and list their responses on the board. Then have students identify which reasons are based on fact and which are based on opinion. Point out to students that when attempting to convince someone of something, it is important to state facts to support your opinion.

2. Explain to students that when writing to persuade, the writer tries to convince the reader(s) that her opinion is the best one. She states her opinion at the beginning; gives details or reasons that prove, explain, or support it; and concludes by restating her opinion.

3. Read aloud the prompt above, display it on a transparency, or write it on the board.

4. Give each student one copy of page 51. Have the student choose her favorite fast-food restaurant from the list on the board and then use the reproducible to organize her thoughts and ideas.

Write It!

1. Instruct each student to use the information recorded on page 51 to help write a paragraph persuading people that her chosen restaurant is the best place to eat. Remind the student to include a topic sentence, at least three strong supporting details, and a concluding sentence. For added fun, encourage each student to use catchy words and phrases in her paragraph (for example: *mouthwatering, delicious, fast, friendly, no hassle, clean,* etc.).

2. Direct the student to proofread and edit her work carefully. Encourage students to swap papers to peer-edit. After all corrections have been made, have each student write her final copy on another sheet of paper or a large index card.

3. If desired, provide each student with a quiet space where she can read aloud her paragraph into a tape recorder, as if she were a radio announcer. Play each recording for the class; then poll students to see which "ad" is the most persuasive!

Persuasive writing

Let's Eat!

My Favorite Restaurant: _____

Topic Sentence: _____

Supporting Details:

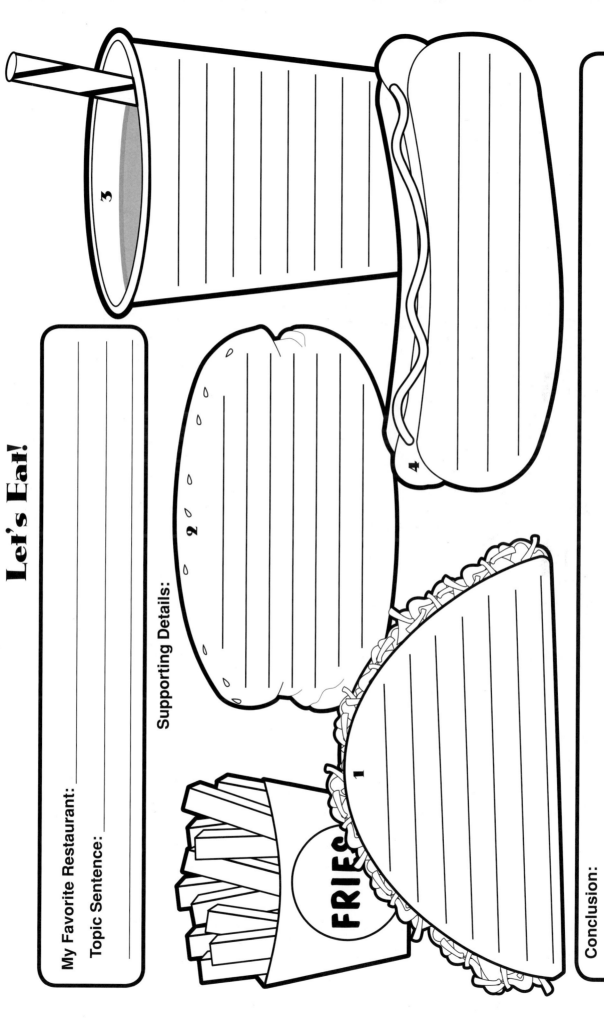

3

2

4

1

FRIES

Conclusion: _____

We're in the Money!

PROMPT *Imagine your family has won a large sum of money, but no one can agree how to spend it! Think of how you would like to spend the money and then write a letter to your family persuading them to agree with you.*

Think It!

1. Ask each student to think of an item—such as a big-screen TV, a stereo system, or a basketball goal—that he would like his family to purchase for their home. Then call on a student volunteer to share his item and reasons why his family should purchase it. For example, a new basketball goal might be the focus of family time and could provide outdoor exercise.

2. Share with students one item that you would like to purchase for your home. Give reasons for your choice, including some facts and some opinions. Point out to students that when attempting to convince someone of something, it is important to state facts to support your opinion.

3. Explain to students that when writing to persuade someone, the writer tries to convince the reader(s) that his opinion is the best one. He states his opinion at the beginning; gives details or reasons that prove, explain, or support it; and concludes by restating his opinion.

4. Read aloud the prompt above, display it on a transparency, or write it on the board.

5. Give each student a copy of page 53. Direct the student to use the reproducible to organize his thoughts and ideas about how his family should spend the money.

Write It!

1. Instruct the student to use the information recorded on page 53 to help write his persuasive letter. Remind the student to include a topic sentence, at least three strong supporting details, and a concluding sentence.

2. Direct the student to proofread and edit his work carefully. Encourage students to swap papers to peer-edit. After all corrections have been made, have the student write his final copy of the letter on a large index card.

3. If desired, punch a hole in each card and then bind the cards with a metal ring. Store the cards in a paper or canvas "money bag" for students to read during free time.

We're in the Money!

Opinion/Topic Sentence:

_____

_____

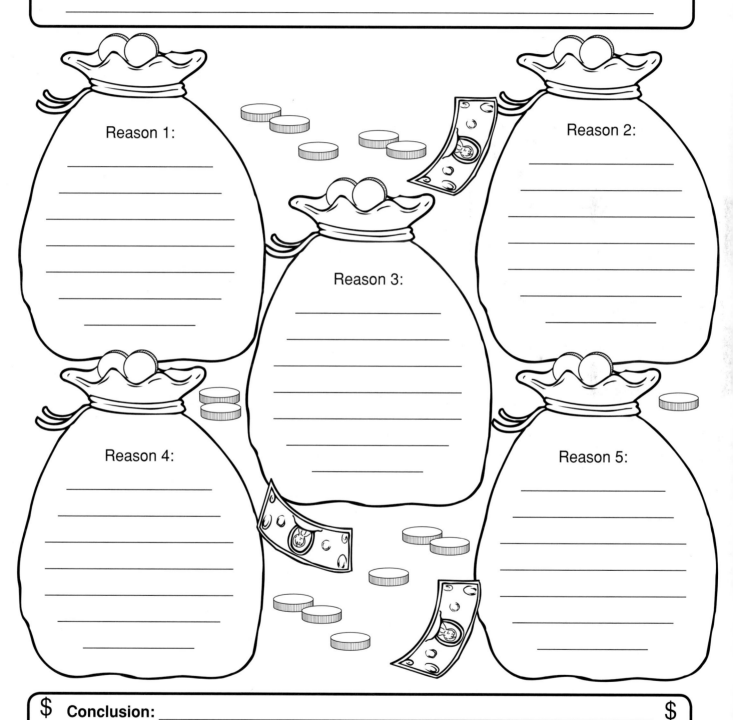

Reason 1:

Reason 2:

Reason 3:

Reason 4:

Reason 5:

$ **Conclusion:** _____ $

_____

$ _____ $

An Invention Convention

PROMPT At the annual Invention Convention, you are asked to head up a committee to select the most important invention of all time. Write a paragraph persuading the committee that the invention you picked is the most important.

Think It!

1. With your students' help, list a few of the greatest inventions of all time on the board (for example, the automobile, lightbulb, and computer). Circle the word *automobile*. Call on several students to share their thoughts about why this invention is important.

2. Write the following sentences about the automobile on the board:
   • The automobile is the most important invention because it makes life easier.
   • The automobile is the most important invention because it can carry people and heavy loads faster than earlier forms of transportation.
   Point out to students that if you were attempting to convince someone that the automobile was the most important invention of all time, it would be important to state facts to support your opinion.

3. Explain to students that when writing to persuade someone, the writer tries to convince the reader(s) that her opinion is the best one. She states her opinion at the beginning; gives details or reasons that prove, explain, or support it; and concludes by restating her opinion.

4. Read aloud the prompt above, display it on a transparency, or write it on the board.

5. Tell each student to select an invention other than the automobile that she thinks is the most important. Give each student a copy of page 55. In the space provided, have the student draw this invention and then use the rest of the reproducible to organize her thoughts and ideas about why it is important.

Write It!

1. Instruct each student to use the information recorded on page 55 to help write her persuasive paragraph on another sheet of paper. Remind the student to include a topic sentence, at least three strong supporting details, and a concluding sentence.

2. Direct the student to proofread and edit her work carefully. Encourage students to swap papers to peer-edit. After all corrections have been made, instruct the student to write her final version on another sheet of paper.

3. If desired, make a large grid using a sheet of chart paper. Post the grid in the center of a bulletin board and display students' final versions around it. As a class, use the grid to make a bar graph showing which inventions were chosen. Then have students (the committee!) use the graph to find out which invention the majority of them thought was the most important.

Invention Convention

The Most Important Invention of All Time

Topic Sentence:

The most important invention of all time is the

_____.

Reason 1:_____

_____

_____

_____

Reason 2:_____

_____

_____

_____

Reason 3:_____

_____

_____

_____

Reason 4:_____

_____

_____

_____

Reason 5:_____

_____

_____

Most important invention? Hmmm...

Conclusion:_____

Cast Your Votes!

PROMPT *Your school is getting ready to hold its annual student council elections, and you've decided to run for office. Write a speech persuading your classmates to vote for you as class president.*

VOTE
TOMMY
FOR
CLASS
PRESIDENT

Think It!

1. Challenge students to recall the names of past or present U.S. presidential candidates. Have them name the good leadership qualities that these candidates possessed. Record their responses on the board.

2. Explain to students that part of running a successful campaign is having a candidate who is able to convince the voters that he or she is the best person for the job. Ask students to determine which of the following is more convincing:
   - When I was leader of my state, it became a better place in which to live.
   - When I was leader of my state, I cut taxes and provided computers for every classroom.
   Point out to students that if they were attempting to convince someone that they would be good leaders, it would be important to state facts to support their opinions.

3. Explain to students that when writing to persuade, the writer tries to convince the reader(s) that his opinion is the best one. He states his opinion at the beginning; gives details or reasons that prove, explain, or support it; and concludes by restating his opinion.

4. Read aloud the prompt above, display it on a transparency, or write it on the board.

5. Give each student a copy of page 57. Instruct the student to use the reproducible to organize his thoughts and ideas for his speech. Encourage him to remember what his classmates thought were the qualities of good leaders—they're the voters!

Write It!

1. Have the student use the information recorded on page 57 to help write his speech. Remind the student to include a topic sentence, at least three strong supporting details, and a concluding sentence.

2. Direct the student to proofread and edit his work carefully. Encourage students to swap papers to peer-edit. After all corrections have been made, have the student write his final copy on another sheet of paper.

3. If desired, have each student read his speech to the rest of the class. Then have the class vote for the most persuasive speech by casting ballots in a mock election. Hail to the chief!

Cast Your Votes!

Opinion/Topic Sentence: _____

_____

Reason 1:   Reason 2:

_____   _____

_____   _____

_____   _____

_____

Reason 3:

VOTE!   _____

                                 _____

                                 _____

                                 _____

Reason 4:   Reason 5:

_____   _____

_____   _____

_____   _____

Conclusion: _____

_____

©The Mailbox® • *Types of Writing* • TEC60930

Are You Ready to Rock?

PROMPT *Your friend has asked you to join a band and it's music to your ears! Write a letter persuading your parents to let you join the band.*

Think It!

1. As a class, brainstorm different kinds of music and favorite bands. Ask students to tell the benefits of being in a band. (For example, it might be fun and they would learn to play an instrument.) List students' responses on the board. Point out to students that if they were attempting to convince someone to let them join a band, it would be important to state facts to support their opinions.

2. Explain to students that when writing to persuade, the writer tries to convince the reader(s) that her opinion is the best one. She states her opinion at the beginning; gives details or reasons that prove, explain, or support it; and concludes by restating her opinion.

3. Read aloud the prompt above, display it on a transparency, or write it on the board.

4. Give each student a copy of page 59. Have her use the top portion of the reproducible to organize her thoughts and ideas.

Write It!

1. Instruct each student to use the information recorded on page 59 to help write a letter persuading her parents to let her join a band. Remind the student to include a topic sentence, at least three strong supporting details, and a concluding sentence.

2. Direct the student to proofread and edit her work carefully. Encourage students to swap papers to peer-edit. After all corrections have been made, have each student write her final copy in the space provided on the bottom portion of page 59.

3. If desired, give each student a 9" x 12" sheet of light-colored construction paper. Direct the student to draw and cut out her favorite musical instrument. Post students' instruments along with their final copies around the room so students can applaud each others' persuasive efforts.

Are You Ready to Rock?

Opinion/Topic Sentence: _____

_____

Supporting Details:

1. _____

_____

2. _____

_____

3. _____

_____

4. _____

_____

Conclusion: _____

_____

©The Mailbox® • *Types of Writing* • TEC60930

_____
_____
_____
_____
_____
_____
_____
_____
_____
_____

©The Mailbox® • *Types of Writing* • TEC60930

Dressing Dilemma

PROMPT

School uniforms—yea or nay? Your principal has asked you to give a speech to the school board about wearing required school uniforms. Write a paragraph persuading the school board to vote for or against this issue.

Think It!

1. Present to your students a school-related issue, such as "School breakfast should be served," or "Students should not change classes for different subjects." Then poll students, asking them to vote yea or nay on the issue.

2. Have student volunteers share their reasons for voting yes or no, listing their responses on the board. Then have students identify the reasons that are factual. Point out to students that when attempting to convince someone of something, it is important to state facts to support your opinion.

3. Explain to students that when writing to persuade, the writer tries to convince the reader(s) that his opinion is the best one. He states his opinion at the beginning; gives details or reasons that prove, explain, or support it; and concludes by restating his opinion.

4. Read aloud the prompt above, display it on a transparency, or write it on the board.

5. Give each student a copy of page 61. Have him use the reproducible to organize his thoughts and ideas about why students should or should not wear school uniforms.

Write It!

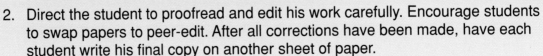

1. Instruct each student to use the information recorded on page 61 to help write his paragraph. Remind the student to include a topic sentence, at least three strong supporting details, and a concluding sentence.

2. Direct the student to proofread and edit his work carefully. Encourage students to swap papers to peer-edit. After all corrections have been made, have each student write his final copy on another sheet of paper.

3. If desired, give each student a sheet of 9" x 12" construction paper and a coat hanger. Direct the student to glue his paragraph to the sheet of construction paper and then tape the paper to the bottom of the hanger. Attach two lengths of string or yarn to a wall, labeling one string "Yea" and the other "Nay." Post students' hangers on the appropriate string.

Dressing Dilemma

BALLOT

Please check one.

I vote ☐ for

☐ against

mandatory school uniforms.

Topic Sentence: _____

_____

Supporting Details:

1

2

3

4

5

Conclusion: _____

_____

Fun With the Family? You Bet!

PROMPT *Your family is going on an outing! Having everyone in your family agree on an activity, however, might take some work. Write a paragraph persuading your family that your idea for family fun is the best one.*

Think It!

1. Have students name some of their favorite things to do with their families (go to a movie, to an amusement park, on a picnic, etc.). Record their responses on the board. Challenge them to give reasons why these activities are so much fun.

2. Tell students what your favorite family activity is. Give reasons why it is your favorite, using facts and opinions. Point out to students that when attempting to convince someone of something, it is important to state facts to support your opinion.

3. Explain to students that when writing to persuade someone, the writer tries to convince the reader(s) that her opinion is the best one. She states her opinion at the beginning; gives details or reasons that prove, explain, or support it; and concludes by restating her opinion.

4. Read aloud the prompt above, display it on a transparency, or write it on the board.

5. Give each student a copy of page 63. Have the student use the reproducible to organize her thoughts and ideas.

Write It!

1. Instruct the student to use the information recorded on page 63 to help write a paragraph persuading her family that her idea for the family outing is the best one. Have her write her paragraph on another sheet of paper. Remind the student to include a topic sentence, at least three strong supporting details, and a concluding sentence.

2. Direct the student to proofread and edit her work carefully. Encourage students to swap papers to peer-edit. After all corrections have been made, have the student write her final copy on a sheet of paper.

3. If desired, give each student a 9" x 12" sheet of white construction paper. Direct the student to draw, color, and cut out a road sign (a rectangle, an inverted triangle, an octagon, etc.). Encourage her to write a fitting phrase on her sign, such as "5 miles to amusement park" or "STOP here for the best restaurant!" Post each student's final copy on a wall or bulletin board, placing her sign atop her paragraph as a cover. Title the display "Fun With the Family? You Bet!"

Name _____

Fun With the Family? You Bet!

**Opinion/
Topic Sentence:**

Supporting Details:

2

1

3

5

4

Conclusion:

May the Best Book Win!

PROMPT *Have you read any good books this year? The Better Books Club is about to present its annual Readers' Choice Award. Write a letter to the club persuading its members that the book you've chosen deserves to be given this honor.*

Think It!

1. Have students name the best books they have recently read. Record their responses on the board. Then have the students give reasons why they like the books.

2. Tell students what your favorite children's book is. Give reasons why it is your favorite, including some facts and opinions. Point out to students that if you were attempting to convince someone that this was the best book, it would be important to state facts to support your opinion.

3. Explain to students that when writing to persuade someone, the writer tries to convince the reader(s) that his opinion is the best one. He states his opinion at the beginning; gives details or reasons that prove, explain, or support it; and concludes by restating his opinion.

4. Read aloud the prompt above, display it on a transparency, or write it on the board. Then give each student a copy of page 65.

5. Direct each student to use the reproducible to organize his thoughts and ideas about his chosen book.

Write It!

1. Tell each student to use the information recorded on page 65 to help write a letter (on another sheet of paper) persuading the club that his book should be given the award. Remind the student to include a topic sentence, at least three strong supporting details, and a concluding sentence.

2. Direct the student to proofread and edit his work carefully. Encourage students to swap papers to peer-edit. After all the corrections have been made, have him write his final draft on another sheet of paper.

3. If desired, give each student a 9" x 12" sheet of white construction paper. Direct the student to fold the sheet in half to create a book jacket. On the front side, have each student title his jacket and illustrate it with a scene or character from his favorite book. Then have him write his finished letter on the inside. Display the finished projects on a covered table with the jackets standing open.

May the Best Book Win!

Book Title: _____

Opinion/Topic Sentence: _____

_____

Supporting Details:

1. _____

2. _____

3. _____

4. _____

5. _____

Conclusion: _____

_____

Trying Television

PROMPT

A study has shown that children spend too much time watching TV. To solve the problem, community leaders are asking parents to turn off the television. Write a paragraph persuading your parents to allow you to watch TV.

Think It!

1. Ask students to estimate the number of hours they spent watching TV last week. Have them list reasons why they think this time was well spent.

2. Tell students that you think people should watch less television. Give reasons why, including some facts and some opinions. Point out to students that when attempting to convince someone of something, it is important to state facts to support your opinion.

3. Explain to students that when writing to persuade someone, the writer tries to convince the reader(s) that his opinion is the best one. He states his opinion at the beginning; gives details or reasons that prove, explain, or support it; and concludes by restating his opinion.

4. Read aloud the prompt above, display it on a transparency, or write it on the board.

5. Give each student a copy of page 67. Have the student use the reproducible to organize his thoughts and ideas.

Write It!

1. Instruct the student to use the information recorded on page 67 to help write a paragraph persuading his parents to allow him to watch TV. Have him write his paragraph on another sheet of paper. Remind the student to include a topic sentence, at least three strong supporting details, and a concluding sentence.

2. Direct the student to proofread and edit his work carefully. Encourage students to swap papers to peer-edit. After all corrections have been made, have the student write his final copy on another sheet of paper.

3. If desired, give each student a 12" x 18" sheet of light-colored construction paper. Instruct the student to glue his paragraph onto the center of the construction paper and then decorate the sheet to look like a TV set (with his paragraph representing the screen). Post the finished projects on a wall or bulletin board titled "Trying Television."

Trying Television

Opinion/Topic Sentence:

_____

_____

_____

Supporting Details:

Conclusion: _____

_____

The Law of the Leash

PROMPT *Several dogs have been running loose around your neighborhood. Your community is hoping to get a leash law passed. Write a letter to community officials persuading them to pass the law.*

Think It!

1. Ask students to list several laws that are in effect in your area *(wearing bike safety helmets, no jaywalking, yielding to pedestrians in crosswalks).* Discuss each law and the possible reasons why it may have been enacted.

2. Write the following sentences on the board:
   - It's good to have a law that requires bicyclists to wear helmets.
   - It's good to have a law that requires bicyclists to wear helmets because helmets protect the head from serious injury.

   Ask students, "If you were trying to convince someone that this law is reasonable, which sentence do you think would be more effective?" Point out to students that sentence two is more effective because a fact is used to support the opinion.

3. Explain to students that when writing to persuade, the writer tries to convince the reader(s) that his opinion is the best one. He states his opinion at the beginning; gives details or reasons that prove, explain, or support it; and concludes by restating his opinion.

4. Read aloud the prompt above, display it on a transparency, or write it on the board.

5. Give each student a copy of page 69. Have the student use the reproducible to organize his thoughts and ideas.

Write It!

1. Direct the student to use the information recorded on page 69 to help write a letter persuading community officials that a leash law should be passed. Remind the student to include a topic sentence, at least three strong supporting details, and a concluding sentence.

2. Direct the student to proofread and edit his work carefully. Encourage students to swap papers to peer-edit. After all corrections have been made, have the student write his final copy of the letter on another sheet of paper.

3. If desired, make an enlarged copy of the dog character on page 69. Have student volunteers create four leashes from construction paper. Attach the character and the leashes to a bulletin board as shown on the reproducible. Post students' letters in clusters at the ends of the leashes.

Name _____

The Law of the Leash

Opinion/Topic Sentence: _____

Reason 1:

Reason 2:

Reason 3:

Reason 4:

Conclusion: _____

Field Trip Fever!

PROMPT *Imagine that you only get one field trip this year. The good news is that you get to decide where you go—and the sky's the limit! But there is one condition: you have to persuade your teacher that your field trip is an educational one!*

Think It!

1. Have your students brainstorm a list of possible sites for a field trip. Record their responses on the board. Have student volunteers give reasons why they like the sites named.

2. Tell students your first choice for a field trip. Give reasons why it's your first choice, including some facts and some opinions. Point out to students that if you were attempting to convince someone that this was the best site, it would be important to state facts to support your opinion.

3. Explain to students that when writing to persuade someone, the writer tries to convince the reader(s) that his opinion is the best one. He states his opinion at the beginning; gives details or reasons that prove, explain, or support it; and concludes by restating his opinion.

4. Read aloud the prompt above, display it on a transparency, or write it on the board.

5. Give each student a copy of page 71. Have the student use the reproducible to organize his thoughts and ideas. Remind him that the reasons he gives for his choice must be educational ones.

Write It!

1. Instruct the student to use the information recorded on page 71 to help write a letter persuading his teacher that his field trip choice is the best one. Have him complete his letter on another sheet of paper. Remind the student to include a topic sentence, at least three strong supporting details, and a concluding sentence.

2. Direct the student to proofread and edit his work carefully. Encourage students to swap papers to peer-edit. After all corrections have been made, have the student write his final copy on another sheet of paper.

3. If desired, gather some items from potential field trip sites, such as brochures, ticket stubs from movies or other events, and playbills. Post these items, along with students' letters, onto a bulletin board. Title the display "Field Trip Fever!"

Persuasive writing

Field Trip Fever!

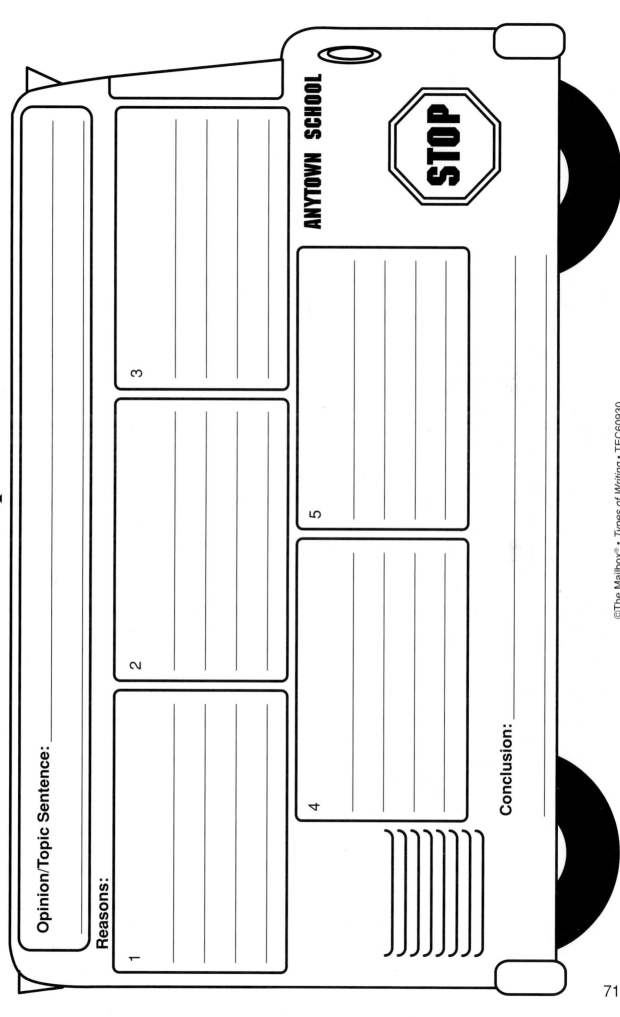

Opinion/Topic Sentence: _____

Reasons:

1

2

3

4

5

Conclusion: _____

ANYTOWN SCHOOL

STOP

Picture-Perfect

You've just returned from an exciting tropical island vacation. The pictures of your trip were damaged. Write a letter to your pen pal, describing the beautiful scenery so vividly that he can picture it in his mind.

Think It!

1. Ask your students to think a moment about their last vacation or trip. Discuss briefly where they went and what they did. List some of the places visited by students on the board.

2. Continue the discussion by talking with students about what kinds of pictures are usually taken on a vacation *(landmarks, scenery, family members, places of interest, wildlife, etc.)*.

3. Read aloud the prompt above, display it on a transparency, or write it on the board. Have students brainstorm a list of things that might be found on the beach of a tropical island *(a hut, white sand, shells, a palm tree, blue water, birds, a crab, boats, etc.)*. List their responses on the board.

4. Give each student a sheet of drawing paper and crayons. Instruct the student to use his imagination to draw the scene of the tropical island beach that he's going to describe in the letter to his pen pal.

Write It!

1. Give each student one copy of page 73. Direct each student to use the left-hand side of the reproducible to record details about what he saw, heard, and smelled on the beach.

2. Then instruct each student to use his illustration and the details recorded on page 73 as a guide to help him write a rough draft of the friendly letter describing the scene to his pen pal.

3. Direct the student to proofread and edit his work carefully. Encourage students to swap papers to peer-edit. After all corrections have been made, have the student write the final copy of his friendly letter on the right-hand side of page 73.

4. Display each student's letter and illustration on a bulletin board titled "Picture-Perfect." Decorate the board with fishing net, shells, shovels, and buckets.

Dear Pen Pal,

Your friend,

_____
(signature)

©The Mailbox® • *Types of Writing* • TEC60930

What I saw: _____

What I heard: _____

What I smelled: _____

©The Mailbox • *Types of Writing* • TEC60930

Toying Around With New Ideas

Tuttle Toy Company, Inc., is looking for the perfect toy designed for kids by a kid. Describe the toy idea you plan to submit. You can describe a brand-new toy or an improvement to an existing toy.

Think It!

1. Have your students brainstorm a list of their favorite toys. Then call on student volunteers to explain what about the particular toys listed makes them so special or fun to play with.

2. Read aloud the prompt above, display it on a transparency, or write it on the board.

3. Give each student one copy of page 75. Then have each student think of an idea for a new toy or an idea for how to improve an existing toy.

4. Instruct the student to draw an illustration of the new toy in the box provided at the top of page 75. Then have the student complete the descriptive word webs at the bottom of the page.

Write It!

1. Have each student use the illustration and the information she records in the word webs on page 75 to help her write two descriptive paragraphs about her new toy.

2. Direct the student to proofread and edit her work carefully. Encourage students to swap papers to peer-edit. After all corrections have been made, have the student write the final copy on another sheet of paper.

3. Display the students' writing on a bulletin board titled "Toying Around With New Ideas!" For a decorative touch, post magazine pictures of various toys around the board.

Toying Around With New Ideas!

Directions: In the box below, draw an illustration of your new or newly improved toy. Then complete each word web at the bottom of the page by filling in descriptive words or phrases that describe or give details about each topic box.

Name of Toy: _____

Descriptive Word Webs

TOPIC
What the Toy Looks Like

TOPIC
How the Toy Can Be Used

What a Dream!

You've just had the strangest dream! In your dream you shrank to the size of an ant for an entire day! Describe how things smelled, sounded, felt, looked, and/or tasted differently being so small. Also describe any dangers you encountered and how you were able to return to your normal size.

Think It!

1. Ask students if any of them have ever seen the movie *Honey, I Shrunk the Kids.* Then ask your students what happened to the kids in the story. (A shrinking machine zapped them to sizes smaller than ants.) Discuss with your students what it must be like to be that small. Have students brainstorm how being so small would make life difficult.

2. Read aloud the prompt above, display it on a transparency, or write it on the board. Then show your students the eraser end of a pencil. Have them imagine being no bigger than the eraser on the end of the pencil when thinking about their stories.

3. Give each student a copy of page 77. Have each student complete each dream bubble on the reproducible before beginning to write his story.

Write It!

1. Instruct each student to use the information recorded in each dream bubble on page 77 to help him write three paragraphs describing the dream: how things smelled, sounded, felt, looked, and/or tasted differently; dangers encountered; and how the student returned to normal size. Remind the student to have a topic sentence and concluding sentence for each paragraph.

2. Allow students time to proofread their work. Next, have students pair up to edit each other's paragraphs. Then instruct each student to write the final version of his story on a separate sheet of paper.

3. For a display, have each student glue his final copy onto the center of a 9" x 12" sheet of light blue construction paper. Then have him trim the outer edges of the construction paper to resemble a dream bubble. Next, give each student a sheet of drawing paper and crayons. Instruct each student to draw a picture of himself sleeping. Post each student's final copy/dream bubble on a bulletin board covered with black bulletin board paper and titled "What a Dream!" Next, post each student's illustration underneath his dream bubble. Tack cotton balls leading from the illustration to the dream bubble to simulate dreaming.

What a Dream!

How things smelled, sounded, felt, looked, and/or tasted:

How you returned to your normal size:

Dangers you encountered:

Serious Cereal

There are dozens of breakfast cereals on the market today. They contain anything from nuts and whole grains to sugar and candy. You've been hired to create a new cereal. Write a descriptive paragraph about your new cereal as it might appear on the back of the cereal box.

Think It!

1. In advance, have each student bring in one empty breakfast cereal box.

2. On the day of this writing activity, display several of the cereal boxes in front of your class for all to see. Then select a few boxes and read aloud the descriptions of the cereals (usually found on the side or back of the box).

3. Have students help you list all the descriptive words used to describe the cereals *(crunchy, complete, fortified, healthy, tasty, etc.)*.

4. Read aloud the prompt above, display it on a transparency, or write it on the board.

5. Inform each student that he is going to create the latest breakfast cereal to be introduced on the market. Further explain that in order to sell the product, he has to write a descriptive paragraph about his new product that will be printed on the cereal box.

Write It!

1. Give each student a copy of page 79. Then instruct the student to complete the word webs on the reproducible by writing a different word in each circle that describes the topic in each box.

2. Instruct each student to use the completed word webs to write a descriptive paragraph about his cereal's taste, texture, nutrition, and uniqueness.

3. Direct the student to proofread and edit his work carefully. Encourage students to swap papers to peer-edit. After all corrections have been made, have the student write the final copy on another sheet of paper.

4. If desired, supply each student with several sheets of construction paper, scissors, glue, and crayons. Instruct the student to cover his cereal box with construction paper. Then have him glue his descriptive paragraph to the front of the box. Next, have him decorate the rest of the box with the name of his cereal and illustrations of his cereal.

5. Tack each student's decorated cereal box to a bulletin board titled "Serious Cereal."

Serious Cereal

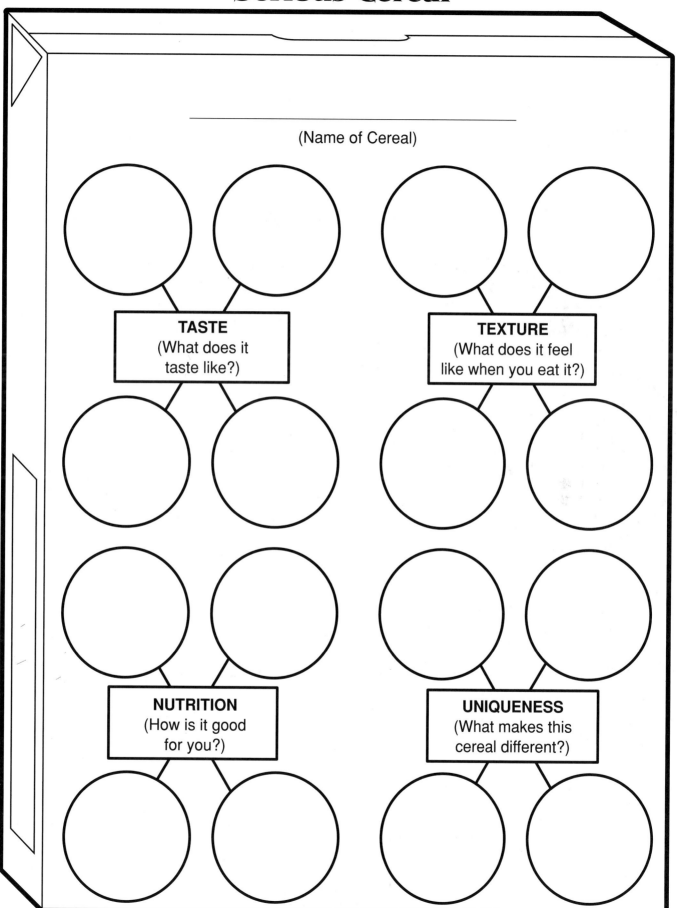

(Name of Cereal)

TASTE
(What does it
taste like?)

TEXTURE
(What does it feel
like when you eat it?)

NUTRITION
(How is it good
for you?)

UNIQUENESS
(What makes this
cereal different?)

Animal Discovery

PROMPT

You are on an African photo safari when you discover an animal that no one has ever seen before! It looks like a combination of two existing animals. You decide to track it. Describe what it looks like, what it eats, and where it lives.

Hello, I'm a lyena.

Think It!

1. Show your students a world map and have them locate the continent of Africa. Then explain to them that a photo *safari* is a trip to see and photograph wild animals. Have your students help you list animals that make their homes in Africa, such as lions, elephants, and hyenas.

2. Read aloud the prompt above, display it on a transparency, or write it on the board.

3. Use the following example to show students how two animals might be combined to create the new animal discovered:
   Example: lion + hyena = lyena or hion

4. Give each student one copy of page 81. Have the student use page 81 to help her organize her thoughts for three descriptive paragraphs about her new discovery.

Write It!

1. Instruct the student to write a rough draft of her description on the back of page 81.

2. Direct the student to proofread and edit her work carefully. Encourage students to swap papers to peer-edit. After all corrections have been made, have the student write the final copy on another sheet of paper.

3. Give each student a large sheet of drawing paper and crayons. Instruct the student to write the name of her new animal discovery at the top of the sheet. Then have her illustrate the creature on the rest of the sheet. Staple the student's writing to the bottom of the illustration; then post all the writings on a board titled "On Safari."

Animal Discovery

_____
(Name of animal)

Where It Lives

Details

What It Eats

Details

What It Looks Like

Details

What a Sight!

You're a tour guide at the local zoo and a reporter from the local newspaper wants to interview you about the three most popular sites or attractions at the zoo. Describe the three popular attractions so that the reporter can write her article.

Think It!

1. Take a poll to see how many students have been to a zoo. Write on the board the names of the zoos visited by students. Then have students brainstorm different sites or attractions found at zoos. Also have students brainstorm what a visitor may see or hear at each site. List their responses on the board.

2. Give each student one copy of page 83. Then read aloud the prompt, display it on a transparency, or write it on the board.

3. Have each student select three zoo sites or attractions to describe. Then have her write the names of the three sites on the graphic organizer (page 83).

4. Direct the student to complete the organizer with words and phrases that describe the sights and sounds of each site.

Write It!

1. On the back of page 83 have each student write descriptive sentences using the words and phrases from her graphic organizer.

2. Direct the student to organize the information into three separate paragraphs—one for each site or attraction. Remind each student to begin the first paragraph with a topic sentence and end the last paragraph with a concluding sentence.

3. Encourage students to edit each other's work and make any needed corrections.

4. Have each student write the final version on another sheet of paper.

5. If desired, give each student one large sheet of construction paper and markers or crayons. Next, instruct the student to fold the paper in half. Have the student paste her writing inside the folded paper. Then instruct her to draw an illustration of one of the described sites on the front of the folded sheet of construction paper. Post the students' work around the classroom for all to enjoy.

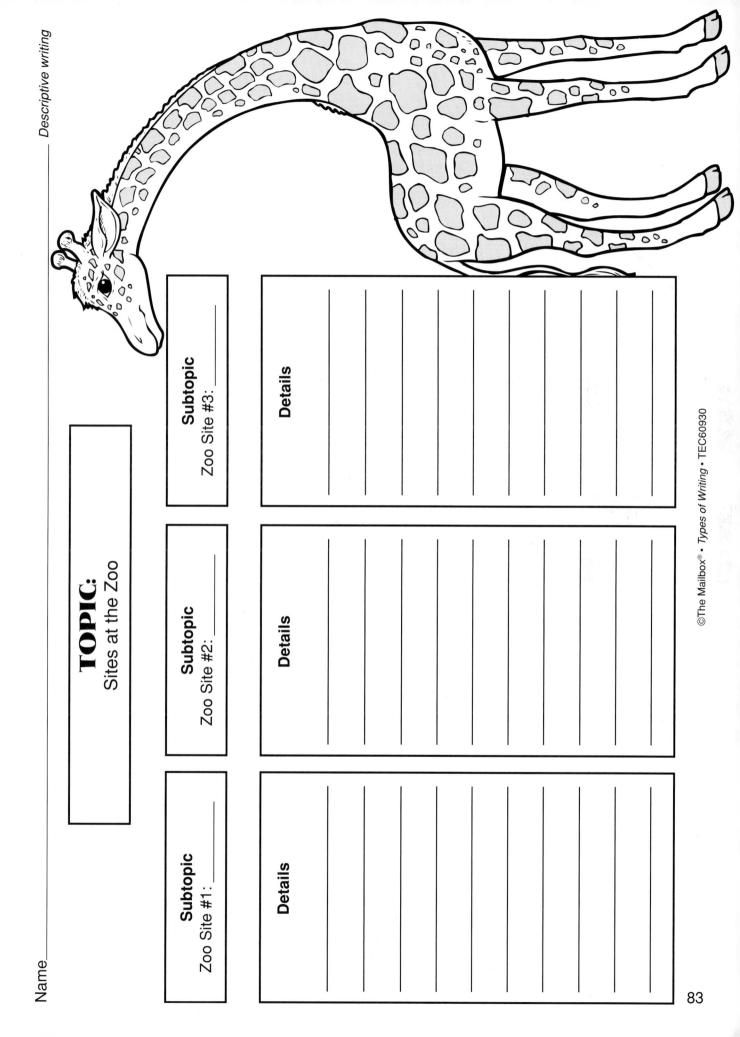

TOPIC:
Sites at the Zoo

Subtopic
Zoo Site #1: _____

Details

Subtopic
Zoo Site #2: _____

Details

Subtopic
Zoo Site #3: _____

Details

"Just the Facts, Ma'am"

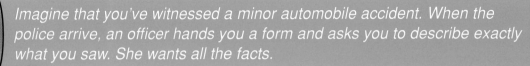

PROMPT *Imagine that you've witnessed a minor automobile accident. When the police arrive, an officer hands you a form and asks you to describe exactly what you saw. She wants all the facts.*

 Think It!

1. Poll students to discover if any of them have ever seen an automobile accident. Select a few student volunteers to briefly describe what they saw. Then brainstorm with the class a list of synonyms for *accident*. List their responses on the board. *(Possible responses: mishap, disaster, emergency, misadventure, calamity)*

2. Give each child a copy of page 85. Then read aloud the prompt above, display it on a transparency, or write it on the board.

3. Before the students begin writing their eyewitness reports, encourage them to think about what the automobiles look like, and what each vehicle did that led up to the collision. Stress to your students the importance of thinking of as many details as possible.

4. After visualizing the crash and the vehicles involved, have each child illustrate the official "photograph" of the accident in the box provided at the top of page 85. Then, on the back of the reproducible, direct each child to list exactly what happened, in the order that it happened.

Write It!

1. Using the information from his list and the official "photograph" as a reference, have each student begin writing his report. Remind him to use order words—such as *first, next,* and *then*—when writing up his report. Also encourage each child to use some of the class-brainstormed synonyms for *accident*.

2. Have students pair up to edit and review each other's "photographs" and reports, checking for details and errors. The police report needs to be as accurate as possible.

3. To create an arresting display with these reports, give each student a manila folder—his case file. Have him glue his police report inside the file. Then write a different case number on the outside of each folder (Case #001, Case #002, etc.) to make them look like official police reports. Mount the reports on a bulletin board titled "Just the Facts, Ma'am" in a way that allows the folders to be easily opened and read by all.

"Just the Facts, Ma'am"

Police Report

(Photograph of the Accident After It Occurred)

Name of Witness: _____

Date and Time of Accident: _____

Location of Accident: _____

Eyewitness Report

_____

_____

_____

_____

_____

_____

_____

_____

_____

_____

_____

_____

_____
Signature and Date

Very Special People

Think of a very special person you know. Describe the qualities that make this person so special.

Think It!

1. Have your students close their eyes and think about the different people in their lives. Suggest to students that they may be thinking of their moms, dads, grandparents, cousins, neighbors, teachers, friends, etc. Then ask each student to think of a person she considers to be very special.

2. Have student volunteers share the special person that came to mind. List their responses on the board. Then read aloud the prompt above, display it on a transparency, or write it on the board.

3. Give each student a copy of page 87. Instruct the student to write the name of her special person in the center of the page and draw an illustration of the special person in the oval above the name. Next, have the student complete the rest of the reproducible with details and information about the special person.

Write It!

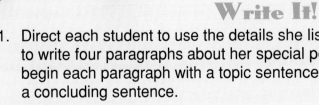

1. Direct each student to use the details she listed in the boxes on page 87 to write four paragraphs about her special person. Remind the student to begin each paragraph with a topic sentence and end each paragraph with a concluding sentence.

2. Direct the student to proofread and edit her work carefully. Encourage students to swap papers to peer-edit. After all corrections have been made, have the student write the final copy on another sheet of paper.

3. Display students' work by posting the writings outside your classroom door for all to enjoy. Title the display "The Special People in Our Lives."

Name ______________________ *Descriptive writing*

Very Special People

Physical traits:

Personality traits:

My Very Special Person

(name)

One special way this person has helped me:

One special way this person has helped others:

The Mysterious Door

PROMPT

After school one day, you return to your class for a book and notice a mysterious door! You open the door and discover it takes you to a magical land. Describe what you see, hear, smell, and feel behind the mysterious door.

Think It!

1. Have your students think of imaginary places they've read about in books or seen in movies or on television, such as Narnia, the settings for Dr. Seuss books, and the Hundred Acre Wood. Have students explain why such places couldn't really exist.

2. Read aloud the prompt above, display it on a transparency, or write it on the board.

3. Give each student one copy of page 89. Instruct each student to use page 89 to help him organize his thoughts and record details about what he sees, hears, smells, and feels behind the mysterious door.

Write It!

1. Instruct each student to write four descriptive paragraphs about her experience behind the mysterious door—one paragraph for each topic on page 89. Remind students to have a topic sentence and concluding sentence for each paragraph.

2. Direct the student to proofread and edit her work carefully. Encourage students to swap papers to peer-edit. After all corrections have been made, have the student write the final copy on another sheet of paper.

3. Give each student a large sheet of white construction paper. Have the student fold it in half like a book cover. Instruct the student to illustrate the magic door on the front of the cover. Then have the student paste her descriptive writing on the inside (right-hand side) of the cover. Display each student's work on and around your classroom door with the heading "The Mysterious Door."

Name ______________________________ *Descriptive writing*

The Mysterious Door

What I saw: ______________________________

What I heard: ______________________________

What I smelled: ______________________________

What I felt: ______________________________

Amazing Amusement Parks

PROMPT *You've just been chosen to design a brochure for the newest amusement park in America! Choose three of the park's best features—such as rides, shows, games, or food—to describe in your brochure.*

Think It!

1. In advance collect several brochures for different attractions in your state or from around the country. AAA (the American Automobile Association) is a good source for such material.

2. Pass the brochures around for all your students to see. Then discuss with your students the characteristics of brochures. *(They usually list just the major aspects of a site, not every detail. They highlight the site's most attractive qualities, and are usually very colorful and eye-catching.)*

3. Read aloud the prompt above, display it on a transparency, or write it on the board.

4. Brainstorm with your students the different areas that might be found in an amusement park, such as rides, places to eat, games, shows, etc.

Write It!

1. Instruct each student to get out one sheet of notebook paper. Then have the student fold the sheet into three equal sections like a brochure. Next have her unfold the sheet and lay it flat on her desk.

2. Direct the student to label the tops of the folded sections with the names of the three amusement park areas she's selected to describe in her brochure. Then instruct the student to use the space below each heading to write a rough draft of the brochure, including as many details as possible.

3. Direct the student to proofread and edit her work carefully. Encourage students to swap papers to peer-edit. After all corrections have been made, give the student a copy of page 91 on which to write and illustrate her final copy.

4. Display the student-made brochures on a bulletin board titled "Amazing Amusement Parks!"

(Name of Amusement Park) _____

(Name of First Area) _____

(Draw illustration here.)

(Name of Second Area) _____

(Draw illustration here.)

(Name of Third Area) _____

(Draw illustration here.)

Created by _____

91

Welcome Home!

PROMPT *Imagine your dream house. Choose a favorite room and describe what it looks like so that someone reading your paper could visualize it.*

Think It!

1. Have students close their eyes while you orally describe a favorite place, such as a restaurant or an outdoor location. Be very detailed with your description. Have students open their eyes; then call on volunteers to recall specific words or phrases that helped them to visualize the place you described.

2. Give each student one copy of page 93. Then, read the prompt above, display it on a transparency, or write it on the board.

3. Challenge each student to draw a detailed picture of his favorite dream-house room on the pattern at the top of the page.

4. Have the student complete the web with words and phrases that describe the room using the five senses. Remind students to use sensory words similar to those you used in your description.

Write It!

1. On the back of his sheet, have each student write descriptive sentences using the words and phrases from his web.

2. Direct the student to organize his sentences into a complete descriptive paragraph, including a topic sentence and concluding sentence. Instruct the student to proof-read and edit his work carefully. Encourage students to swap papers to peer-edit. After all corrections have been made, have the student write his paragraph on a separate sheet of paper.

3. If desired, have each student cut out his illustration and paragraph and paste them onto a colorful sheet of 12" x 18" construction paper. Display the completed projects on a bulletin board titled "Welcome Home!"

Welcome Home!

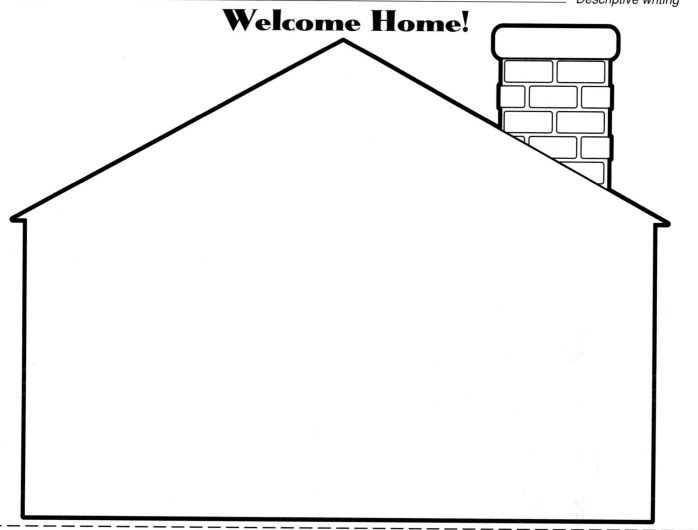

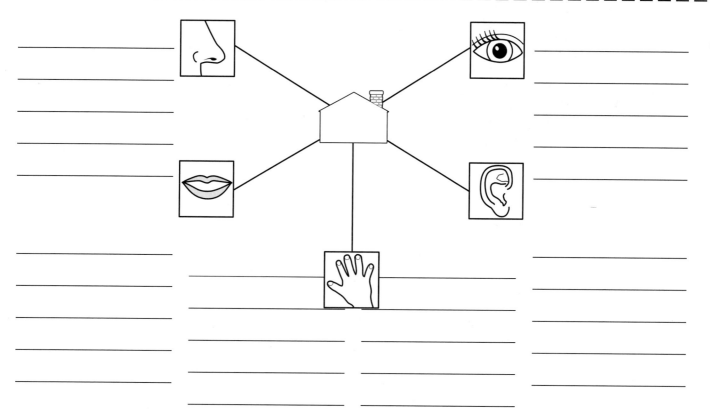

Treasure Trek

PROMPT

Imagine that a treasure is discovered hidden somewhere in your school and you are the only one who knows where it is. Write a paragraph explaining how to find the treasure.

SCHOOL TREASURE MAP

Think It!

1. Draw a rough sketch of your school on the board. Then explain how to get from your classroom to another area of the school, using the sketch you drew. As you explain, be sure to use transitional and linking words, as well as directional words, to help students understand your instructions.

2. Read aloud the prompt above, display it on a transparency, or write it on the board.

3. Have each student use the map you drew on the board to select a location in the school for the hidden treasure. Then give each student a copy of page 95 and instruct him to draw his own map of the school, including a key or legend.

Write It!

1. On another sheet of paper, have the student write a paragraph giving directions for finding the hidden treasure. Remind him that he is writing to explain and should use transitional or linking words. Also remind him to include a topic sentence and a concluding sentence in his paragraph.

2. Direct the student to proofread and edit his work carefully. Encourage students to swap papers to peer-edit.

3. After all corrections have been made, instruct each student to write his final copy on the bottom of page 95.

4. If desired, have students exchange papers and go on a treasure hunt to check the directions. Display students' maps and final copies on a bulletin board titled "Our Treasure Trek!"

Treasure Trek

School Treasure Map

Map Key

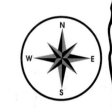

_____

(Title)

_____
_____
_____
_____
_____
_____
_____
_____
_____
_____
_____

Crafty Creations

PROMPT *Think about your favorite arts-and-crafts project. Write one or more paragraphs explaining how to make this project so a friend could make it too!*

Think It!

1. Share with students an arts-and-crafts project that you or someone you know has created. Explain the steps for making this project. Examples may include crocheting an afghan or building a model.

2. Ask student volunteers to describe arts-and-crafts projects they have made or seen someone else make. List the projects on the board.

3. Read aloud the prompt above, display it on a transparency, or write it on the board. Then give each student a copy of page 97.

4. In the space provided, instruct each student to list the supplies needed to complete her project. Challenge the student to use the list she made to help her explain the steps needed to make her project.

Write It!

1. Instruct each student to use the information recorded on page 97 to write one or more paragraphs on another sheet of paper. Remind her that she is writing to explain and should use transitional or linking words. Also remind her to include a topic sentence and a concluding sentence in her paragraph(s).

2. Direct the student to proofread and edit her work carefully. Encourage students to swap papers to peer-edit. After all corrections have been made, have the student write her final draft on a separate sheet of paper.

3. If desired, combine all of the final copies into a class book titled "Our Class's Crafty Creations!"

Name ____________________

My Crafty Creation

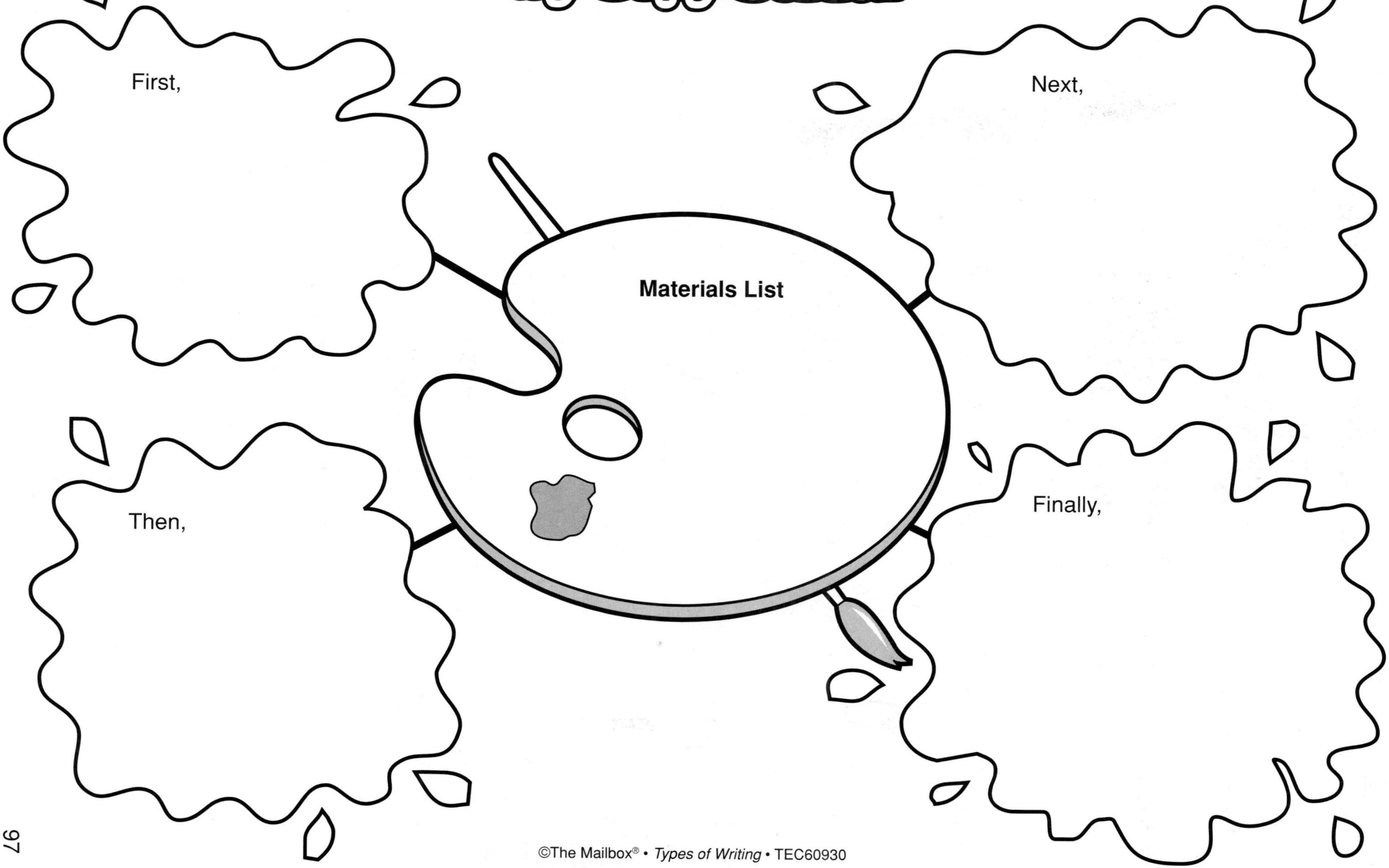
First,
Next,
Materials List
Then,
Finally,

There's No Place Like Home!

PROMPT

Imagine that you are going to ride a different bus home from school. Write a paragraph for the bus driver explaining how to get to your home.

Think It!

1. Share with students the route you take to get from school to your house each day. Use directional words—such as *north, south, right,* or *left*—and include landmarks—such as special buildings or colorful houses—to help students visualize your directions. Then ask students what would happen if you were giving someone these directions and you left out one of the steps.

2. Direct each student to close his eyes and visualize the route from school to his home. Then read aloud the prompt above, display it on a transparency, or write it on the board.

3. Give each student a copy of page 99. In the first column on the chart, instruct the student to list all of the streets the bus driver will need to turn onto to get from the school to his home. In the second and third columns, challenge the student to write directional words the bus driver will need to know to turn onto each street and any landmarks she will see.

4. Instruct the student to use the information in the chart to help him write directions on the house shape explaining how to get to his home from school.

Write It!

1. On another sheet of paper, have the student use the information recorded on the reproducible to write a paragraph explaining how to get from school to his home. Remind the student that he is writing to explain and should use transitional or linking words. Also remind him to include a topic sentence and a concluding sentence in his paragraph.

2. Direct the student to proofread and edit his work carefully. Encourage students to swap papers to peer-edit. After all corrections have been made, direct the student to write his final copy on another sheet of paper.

3. If desired, give each student a 9" x 12" sheet of construction paper. On one side have the student draw and color a picture of his home; then have him glue his final copy onto the other side. Using a length of string, hang each student's picture from the ceiling and label the display "There's No Place Like Home!"

There's No Place Like Home!

Name of the Street	Direction to Turn	Helpful Landmarks

First, _____

_____

_____

Next, _____

_____

_____

Then, _____

_____

_____

Finally, _____

_____

Just Plane Directions!

PROMPT *Think about the last time you made a paper airplane, how you made it, and how well it flew. Write a paragraph explaining how to make a paper airplane from a sheet of loose-leaf paper.*

Think It!

1. Have each student take out a sheet of loose-leaf paper. Challenge each student to make a paper airplane from the sheet. Encourage the student to pay close attention to each step as she creates the plane.

2. Read aloud the prompt above, display it on a transparency, or write it on the board. Then give each student a copy of page 101.

3. Instruct each student to use the spaces provided on the reproducible to sketch the steps she followed to make her paper airplane. Encourage the student to make another plane as she draws, if necessary. Direct the student to draw more boxes on the back of the page, if needed.

4. Below each sketch, have the student write a sentence explaining that step.

Write It!

1. On another sheet of paper, have the student use the information recorded on page 101 to write a paragraph, including a topic sentence and a concluding sentence. Remind the student that she is writing to explain and should use transitional or linking words to make the steps easier to follow.

2. Direct the student to proofread and edit her work carefully. Encourage students to swap papers to peer-edit. After all corrections have been made, have the student write her final copy on another sheet of paper.

3. After writing her final copy, have the student exchange paragraphs with a classmate and follow the directions as written to make a paper airplane. Then take students outside to test the planes. If desired, display planes and final copies on a bulletin board titled "Just Plane Directions!"

Just Plane Directions!

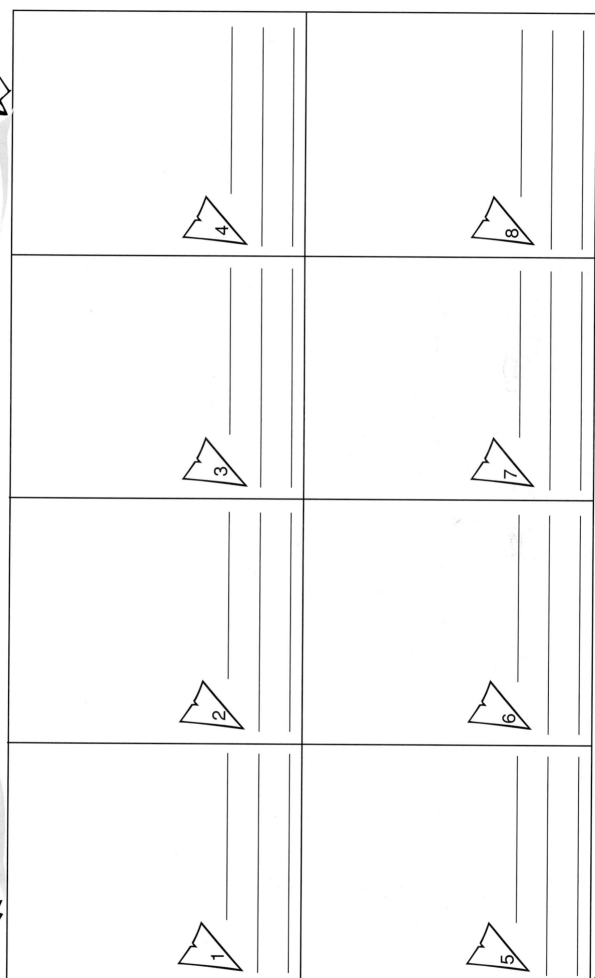

It's All Fun and Games!

PROMPT *Think about your favorite inside game and how it is played. Write one or more paragraphs explaining the directions for this game so your best friend will be able to play it with you.*

rattle rattle

Think It!

1. Ask students to think about a time when they played an inside game that was new to them, such as dominoes, checkers, or a board game. Point out the importance of having directions, whether written or verbal, to learn the rules of a new game.

2. Read aloud the prompt above, display it on a transparency, or write it on the board. Then give each student a copy of page 103.

3. Direct each student to use the top of page 103 to list the materials needed to play his favorite game. Then have the student think about the steps required to play his game. Challenge him to list these steps in the space provided.

4. Have the student read over his directions and number them in the order in which they should be followed.

Write It!

1. Instruct each student to use the information recorded on page 103 to write one or more paragraphs explaining how to play his game. Have the student write his paragraph(s) on another sheet of paper. Remind him that he is writing to explain and should use transitional or linking words. Also remind him to include a topic sentence and a concluding sentence in his paragraph(s).

2. Direct the student to proofread and edit his work carefully. Encourage students to swap papers to peer-edit. After all corrections have been made, have the student write his final copy on another sheet of paper.

3. If desired, place each student's directions in a folder labeled with the title of his game. Allow students to bring in their favorite games from home. Place the folders and games at a center. Have students select a game to test and play with a classmate during free time.

It's All Fun and Games!

Game Materials

_____ _____

_____ _____

_____ _____

_____ _____

Steps to Play My Game

☐ _____

☐ _____

☐ _____

☐ _____

☐ _____

☐ _____

☐ _____

☐ _____

Wishing Our Chores Away

PROMPT *Imagine that you have been granted one wish by a genie. You tell the genie that you would like him to do your least favorite household chore. Write a paragraph for the genie, explaining how to do your chore correctly.*

Think It!

1. Share with students your least favorite household chore and why you dislike it. Ask student volunteers to share their least favorite chore and what they dislike about it. For example, a student might say she dislikes vacuuming because her house is all carpeted and it takes her a long time to complete the chore.

2. Read aloud the prompt above, display it on a transparency, or write it on the board. Then give each student a copy of page 105.

3. At the top of page 105, have the student list the steps the genie will need to follow to successfully complete the chore.

4. Instruct the student to read over what she has written and number her steps in the order in which they should be completed.

Write It!

1. On another sheet of paper, have the student use the information on page 105 to write a paragraph explaining how to complete her least favorite chore. Remind the student that she is writing to explain and should use transitional or linking words. Also remind her to include a topic sentence and a concluding sentence in her paragraph.

2. Direct the student to proofread and edit her paper carefully. Encourage students to swap papers to peer-edit.

3. After all corrections have been made, instruct the student to write her final draft in the space provided on page 105. Then have students cut out their final drafts along the bold line.

4. If desired, in advance, ask students to bring in cleaned small plastic soda bottles. Have each student decorate her "magic wishing bottle" with arts-and-crafts supplies. Then have her roll up her final draft and put it into the bottle, leaving enough of the paper sticking out for someone to be able to get it to read. Display the bottles, then title the display "Wishing Our Chores Away."

Wishing Our Chores Away

Steps to Complete My Chore

_____

_____

_____

_____

_____

_____

_____

_____

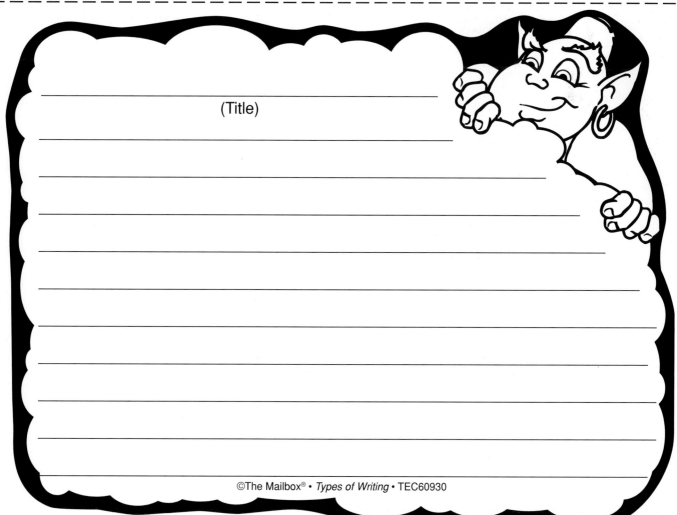

_____
(Title)

Order Up!

PROMPT *Imagine that a visitor from another country is staying with your family. You want to take him to a fast-food restaurant, but he has never been to one. Write a paragraph for the visitor explaining how to order a meal in a fast-food restaurant.*

Think It!

1. Instruct each student to close his eyes and think about the last time he went to a fast-food restaurant. Have him retrace his steps from the time he entered the restaurant until the time he was served his food.

2. Ask student volunteers to share their experiences with the class.

3. Read aloud the prompt above, display it on a transparency, or write it on the board. Then give each student a copy of page 107.

4. At the top of page 107, have each student write the steps a person must follow to order a meal in a fast-food restaurant.

Write It!

1. On a sheet of paper, have the student write a paragraph explaining how to order a fast-food meal using the information recorded on page 107. Remind him to use transitional or linking words and to include a topic sentence and a concluding sentence.

2. Direct the student to proofread and edit his work carefully. Encourage students to swap papers to peer-edit.

3. After all corrections have been made, have the student write his final copy on the hamburger pattern at the bottom of page 107.

4. If desired, have each student cut out his completed paragraph and display it on a bulletin board titled "Order Up!"

Order Up!

First, _____

_____

Next, _____

_____

Then, _____

_____

Finally, _____

_____

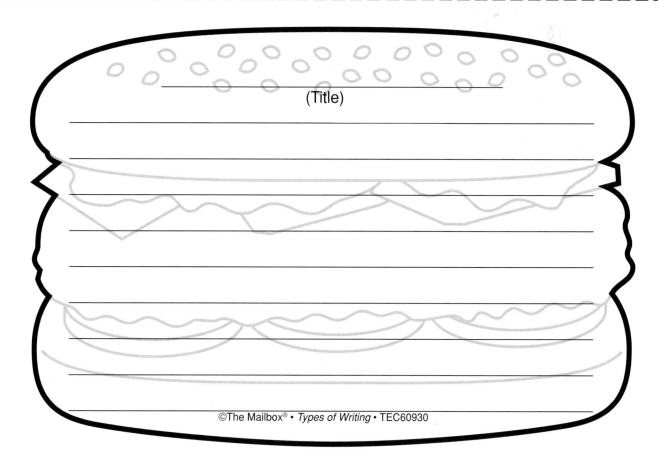

(Title)

_____

_____

_____

_____

_____

Math Made Easy

PROMPT *Imagine that you have been asked to explain to a classmate how to solve a math problem. Write a paragraph giving detailed instructions explaining how to solve this problem.*

6,000
− 593
?

362
× 79
?

Think It!

1. Ask students to think about the first time they learned how to add, subtract, multiply, or divide. Point out how important it was for them to get clear directions when learning the math operations.

2. Read aloud the prompt above, display it on a transparency, or write it on the board. Then give each student a copy of page 109.

3. At the top of page 109, have the student write a challenging math problem, such as a word problem, multiplying a double-digit number by a double-digit number, or subtracting with zeros.

4. Below this, have the student list the steps needed to solve the problem. Then have him number the steps in the order in which they should be followed.

Write It!

1. On another sheet of paper, have the student use the information recorded on page 109 to write a paragraph on how to solve his problem. Remind the student that he is writing to explain and should include transitional or linking words. Also remind him to include a topic sentence and a concluding sentence in his paragraph.

2. Direct the student to proofread and edit his work carefully. Encourage students to swap papers to peer-edit.

3. After all corrections have been made, have the student write his final draft in the space provided on page 109.

4. If desired, allow each student to cut out his final draft and exchange his paper with a partner to test the directions. Then display them on a bulletin board titled "Math Made Easy."

Math Made Easy

_____
(Title)

Problem to Solve:

Steps for Solving the Problem:

109

Critter Sitters

PROMPT *Imagine you are going out of town for a weekend and have asked a friend to care for your pet while you're gone. Write one or more paragraphs to your friend, explaining how to care for your pet.*

Think It!

1. Ask a student volunteer to share a time when he was asked to care for a pet. On the board, list the tasks or types of things the student did to care for the pet.

2. Read aloud the prompt above, display it on a transparency, or write it on the board. Then give each student a copy of page 111.

3. Have each student choose a real or imaginary pet he would like his friend to care for while he is gone. Have the student draw a picture of the pet in the first box.

4. In the second box, have the student list the animal's needs and supplies, such as food, exercise, and shelter.

5. In the last box on page 111, have the student write the steps explaining how to care for his pet.

Write It!

1. On another sheet of paper, have the student use the information recorded on page 111 to write detailed pet care instructions for his friend. Remind the student that he is writing to explain and should use transitional or linking words. Also remind him to include a topic sentence and a concluding sentence in his paragraph(s).

2. Direct the student to proofread and edit his work carefully. Encourage students to swap papers to peer-edit. After all corrections have been made, instruct the student to write his final copy on a separate sheet of paper.

3. If desired, display students' final copies on a bulletin board covered in newspaper titled "Critter Sitters!"

Critter Sitters

MY PET

NEEDS AND SUPPLIES

_____ _____

_____ _____

_____ _____

_____ _____

_____ _____

PET CARE INSTRUCTIONS

First, _____

_____

_____

Next, _____

_____

_____

Then, _____

_____

_____

Finally, _____

_____

_____

Student for Hire!

PROMPT *Imagine that you want to find a job in your neighborhood to earn some extra money. Think about the job that you will do. Write a paragraph explaining the steps you will need to take in order to get this job.*

Think It!

1. Ask students to name some of the jobs students their age can do to raise money. For example, they could run a lemonade stand, mow lawns, baby-sit, help paint fences, or wash cars.

2. Discuss with students the types of things they should consider when preparing for a job. For example, they should think about what supplies they will need, any safety issues that may be involved, when they will do the job and how often, and how much they will charge.

3. Read aloud the prompt above, display it on a transparency, or write it on the board. Then give each student a copy of page 113.

4. Direct the student to use the reproducible to help her organize her thoughts and ideas for planning her job.

Write It!

1. On another sheet of paper, have the student use the information recorded on page 113 to write one or more paragraphs about how she plans to get a job to raise money. Remind her that she is writing to explain and should use transitional and linking words. Also remind her to include a topic sentence and a concluding sentence in her paragraph(s).

2. Direct the student to proofread and edit her work carefully. Encourage students to swap papers to peer-edit. After all corrections have been made, have the student write her final draft on a separate sheet of paper.

3. If desired, cover a bulletin board with classified ads from the newspaper. Post students' final drafts on the board. Title it "Students for Hire!"

Name _____

Student for Hire!

Lemonade 25¢

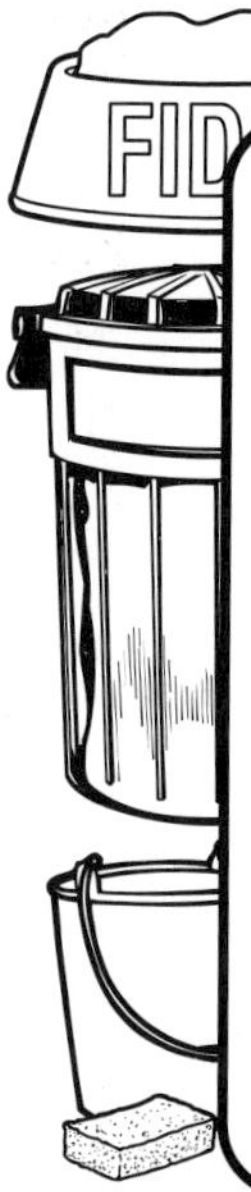

1. What job will I do? _____

2. What supplies will I need? _____

   _____

3. What safety issues should I be concerned about? _____

   _____

4. How much time will the job take? _____

5. When will I do the job? _____

6. How much will I charge? _____

Steps to Take to Get My Job:

First, _____

_____

_____

Next, _____

_____

_____

Then, _____

_____

_____

Finally, _____

_____

_____

Snack to It!

PROMPT *Imagine you are getting ready for an upcoming sleepover at your house. You want your mom to make your favorite snack for you and your friends. Write a paragraph for your mom explaining how to make the snack.*

Think It!

1. Ask students to imagine what would happen if a baker iced a cake before he put it in the oven or a butcher wrapped up meat before he cut it. Brainstorm with students other activities in which following sequential directions is important.

2. Read aloud the prompt above, display it on a transparency, or write it on the board.

3. Give each student a copy of page 115. Direct the student to list all of the ingredients and supplies he will need on the recipe card at the top of the page.

4. At the bottom of the page, have the student write the steps needed to make his snack. Encourage the student to include serving suggestions, such as serves four people, place in a bowl with the crackers on the side, or arrange so the colors alternate.

Write It!

1. On another sheet of paper, have the student use the information recorded on page 115 to write a paragraph giving instructions on how to make his favorite snack. Remind the student that he is writing to explain and should use transitional or linking words. Also remind him to include a topic sentence and a concluding sentence in his paragraph.

2. Direct the student to proofread and edit his work carefully. Encourage students to swap papers to peer-edit.

3. After all corrections have been made, instruct each student to write his final copy on a recipe card made from half of a file folder. If desired, create a class recipe book titled "Snack to It!"

Name _____

Snack to It!

My Favorite Snack

Ingredients and Supplies

_____
_____
_____
_____
_____
_____
_____
_____

Steps for Making My Snack

First, _____
_____
_____

Next, _____
_____
_____

Then, _____
_____
_____

Finally, _____
_____
_____

Extra Prompts

1. Decision making is a part of everyone's life. Some decisions are easier to make than others. Write about a time you had to make a difficult decision.

2. Everyone can play a part in helping the less fortunate in their community. Write a story about how you might like to help out someone in your community who is in need.

3. Everyone's family is unique and special. Write a story about a special memory of your family that shows just how special it really is.

4. Imagine you've just inherited enough money to buy the home of your dreams. Write a story about winning the money and buying your dream house.

5. What is your neighborhood like? Is it a quiet street with homes that look like yours? Or is it noisy and busy? Tell about a typical day in your neighborhood.

6. Everybody has a favorite food. Imagine that you've just won a trip to visit the factory where your favorite food is made. Write a story about your trip.

7. An autobiography is your life history—where and when you were born, your family, important things you've done, etc. Try your hand at writing a short autobiography.

8. You've just discovered that one of your relatives is a famous movie star. Write a story about being invited to visit your famous relative.

9. School projects can be a great way to learn and great fun! Tell a story about a school project you were proud of and particularly enjoyed completing.

10. Pretend that you have received a letter from a pen pal asking you to visit him/her but that you are unable to go. Write a response to this friend, telling about the situation that is keeping you from visiting.

Extra Prompts

1. Your parents are buying a brand-new automobile! They want your opinion about which one to buy—a luxury car, a minivan, or a sport-utility vehicle. Write a paragraph to your parents persuading them to buy one of the vehicles.

2. Your friends are all getting their own personal telephones, but your parents think it is a waste of money. Write a letter to your parents persuading them to let you get a phone of your own.

3. Your grade-level classmates are hosting a school dance. They can't decide which musical group to invite to perform. Write a paragraph persuading your classmates to choose your favorite group.

4. The local humane society is trying to get citizens to adopt some of its animals. Write a persuasive paragraph promoting the adoption of these pets. Give reasons that explain the advantages of adopting a pet.

5. You and your friends want to get together this weekend. The only problem is, you can't agree on what to do. Choose an activity; then write a letter to your friends convincing them to agree with you.

6. Summer is here and you want to get a job to earn a little extra spending money. But your parents aren't quite sure they want to allow you to do this. Write a paragraph to your parents persuading them to let you get a summertime job.

7. The mayor of your city is trying to decide if a 7:00 P.M. curfew for children under the age of 14 is needed. What do you think? Write a letter to the mayor to convince him or her to enact, or not to enact, the curfew.

8. Your normal bedtime is 9:30 P.M. There is a 10:00 movie that you want to see tonight. Write a paragraph persuading your parents to let you stay up and watch the movie.

9. In order to save money, your principal is thinking about canceling all field trips for the remainder of the year! Write a letter to your principal persuading him or her to allow students to continue taking field trips.

Extra Prompts

1. Pick an outside location, maybe the park, a baseball field, your backyard, etc. In three paragraphs, describe in detail what you hear, see, and smell.

2. Imagine that you have the most unusual pet in the whole town. Describe your pet and what makes it so unusual and unique.

3. Imagine you are an explorer and have just discovered an uncharted island. Describe your discovery so that your friends back home can picture the island in their minds.

4. You've left an important assignment in a shoebox in your closet at home. You are on the phone trying to describe the shoebox to your mom. The problem is that there are five different shoeboxes in your closet. Describe in detail the one shoebox that contains your assignment.

5. Everyone has a favorite outfit. Write a paragraph describing your favorite outfit, from your head to your toes!

6. Your school is having a flag-design contest to select a new school flag. You've decided to enter the contest. Describe in detail what your flag will look like.

7. You and your best friend stumble upon a buried treasure chest. As you open the chest you are amazed at the riches inside! Describe the contents of the chest.

8. You've won the grand prize from Playground Equipment, Inc. This entitles you to any playground setup of your choice. Describe in detail the new equipment for your new playground.

9. Have a sweet tooth? Describe your favorite candy bar. Include the main ingredients and describe whether the bar is crunchy, chewy, or gooey.

10. No one knows you better than yourself. Write two descriptive paragraphs about yourself. In the first paragraph, describe your physical characteristics (what you look like). In the second paragraph, describe your personality.

Extra Prompts

1. Imagine that you're preparing for a bubble-blowing contest. Write a paragraph explaining how to blow the biggest bubble with chewing gum.

2. Who ever said that you can't teach an old dog a new trick? Write a letter to the American Kennel Club explaining how to teach a dog a trick.

3. Who doesn't like to make new friends? Imagine that you are going on the radio to tell people how to do this. Write a paragraph explaining what you'd say.

4. Washing a car is a great way to earn extra money. Write an advertisement that includes an explanation of how to wash a car.

5. Your best friend wants advice on how to study for a test. Write a note to your friend explaining how to do this.

6. It's your turn to clean up the dinner dishes, but you have been invited to eat at a friend's house. Your little brother has volunteered to do the dishes for you. Write a note to your brother explaining how to do this.

7. Your mom has asked your older cousin to drive you to the grocery store. Your cousin doesn't know how to get to the store. Write a paragraph for your cousin explaining how to get from your house to the grocery store.

8. You and your family are going on vacation. Your little sister wrote you a note telling you that she doesn't know how to pack a suitcase! Write a response to your sister explaining how to do this.

9. Ah, the thought of a picnic on a perfect summer day. Imagine that you've invited a friend on a picnic. Then write a letter to your friend explaining how you will prepare for this event.

10. It's almost time for your six-month dental checkup. Your dentist calls you and asks that you be prepared to explain how to correctly brush your teeth! Write a note to your dentist explaining how to do this.

Proofreading Checklist

To the Student: Use this checklist during the proofreading or editing stage of your writing to help you determine what needs improving and/or correcting before writing the final version. Then give this checklist and your writing to a peer editor (a classmate) to use to edit your work.

Title of Writing Selection:_____

Things to Check	Writer's Checklist		Peer Editor's Checklist	
	Yes	No	Yes	No
1. Does the writing have a beginning in which characters and setting are introduced?				
2. Does the writing have a middle that reveals the problem or action of the story?				
3. Does the writing have an ending that contains the solution to the problem or conclusion to the activity?				
4. Does the writing make sense, and is it easy to read?				
5. Did the writer use descriptive words?				
6. Did the writer make use of transition words such as *next, then, first, however,* and *furthermore?*				
7. Does each sentence begin with a capital letter?				
8. Does each sentence have an ending punctuation mark?				
9. Did the writer use complete sentences?				
10. Did the writer check for misspelled words?				
11. Is each paragraph indented?				

☆ If the peer editor checked "No" in any box above, discuss it with the editor.

Think About It!

I think I did a _____ job on this writing selection because…

_____

_____

Narrative-Writing Assessment

Student's Name: _____   **Date:** _____

Title of Writing: _____

Assessment Items	Agree	Disagree
1. The writing selection contains a beginning in which characters and setting are introduced.		
2. The writing selection contains a middle that reveals the problem or action of the story.		
3. The writing selection has an ending that contains the solution to the problem or conclusion to the activity.		
4. Descriptive words and sensory details are used.		
5. The writing selection makes sense; it is easy to read.		
6. Information and details are presented in a logical order.		
7. Transition words—such as *next, then, first, however,* and *furthermore*—are used.		
8. All details relate to the topic.		
9. Correct punctuation is used.		
10. Each word is spelled correctly.		
11. Run-on sentences and incomplete sentences are avoided.		
12. Each verb agrees with its subject.		
13. All proper nouns are capitalized.		
14. Each paragraph is indented.		
15. Apostrophes are correctly used to form contractions and to show possession.		

Comments: _____

_____

_____

_____

Proofreading Checklist

To the Student: Use this checklist during the proofreading or editing stage of your writing to help you determine what needs improving and/or correcting before writing the final version. Then give this checklist and your writing to a peer editor (a classmate) to use to edit your work.

Title of Writing Selection:_____

Things to Check	Writer's Checklist		Peer Editor's Checklist	
	Yes	No	Yes	No
1. Does the writing have a topic sentence and a concluding sentence?				
2. Does the writing clearly state the opinion?				
3. Do the details or reasons prove, explain, or support the opinion?				
4. Are any of the details or reasons used factual?				
5. Does the writing make sense and is it easy to read?				
6. Did the writer use strong nouns, adjectives, and verbs?				
7. Does each sentence begin with a capital letter?				
8. Does each sentence have an ending punctuation mark?				
9. Did the writer use complete sentences?				
10. Did the writer check for misspelled words?				
11. Is each paragraph indented?				

☆ If the peer editor checked "No" in any box above, discuss it with the editor.

Think About It!

I think I did a _____ job on this writing selection because…

_____

_____

Persuasive-Writing Assessment

Student's Name: _____ **Date:** _____

Title of Writing: _____

Assessment Items	Agree	Disagree
1. The writing selection has a topic sentence and concluding sentence.		
2. The writing selection persuades someone of something.		
3. The topic sentence clearly states an opinion.		
4. The details or reasons prove, explain, or support the opinion.		
5. Factual details are used.		
6. All details relate to the topic.		
7. The writing selection makes sense; it is easy to read.		
8. Strong nouns, adjectives, and verbs are used.		
9. Correct punctuation and capitalization are used.		
10. Each word is spelled correctly.		
11. Run-on sentences and incomplete sentences are avoided.		
12. Each verb agrees with its subject.		
13. All proper nouns are capitalized.		
14. Each paragraph is indented.		
15. Apostrophes are correctly used to form contractions and to show possession.		

Comments: _____

_____

_____

_____

_____

Proofreading Checklist

To the Student: Use this checklist during the proofreading or editing stage of your writing to help you determine what needs improving and/or correcting before writing the final version. Then give this checklist and your writing to a peer editor (a classmate) to use to edit your work.

Title of Writing Selection:_____

Things to Check	Writer's Checklist		Peer Editor's Checklist	
	Yes	No	Yes	No
1. Does the writing have an introduction, a body, and a conclusion?				
2. Does the writing make sense and is it easy to read?				
3. Did the writer use descriptive words?				
4. Does each sentence begin with a capital letter?				
5. Does each sentence have an ending punctuation mark?				
6. Did the writer use complete sentences?				
7. Did the writer check for misspelled words?				
8. Is each paragraph indented?				
9. Does each paragraph contain a topic sentence?				
10. Does each paragraph contain a concluding sentence?				
11. Do all the details stick to the topic?				

☆ If the peer editor checked "No" in any box above, discuss it with the editor.

Think About It!

I think I did a _____ job on this writing selection because…

_____

_____

Descriptive-Writing Assessment

Student's Name: _____ **Date:** _____

Title of Writing: _____

Assessment Items	Agree	Disagree
1. Descriptive words and sensory details are used.		
2. The writing selection makes sense; it is easy to read.		
3. The writing selection has an introduction, a body, and a conclusion.		
4. Information and details are presented in a logical order.		
5. All details relate to the topic.		
6. Correct punctuation is used.		
7. Each sentence begins with a capital letter.		
8. Each word is spelled correctly.		
9. Run-on sentences and incomplete sentences are avoided.		
10. Each paragraph contains a topic sentence.		
11. Each paragraph contains a concluding sentence.		
12. Each verb agrees with its subject.		
13. All proper nouns are capitalized.		
14. Each paragraph is indented.		
15. Apostrophes are correctly used to form contractions and to show possession.		

Comments: _____

_____

_____

_____

Proofreading Checklist

To the Student: Use this checklist during the proofreading or editing stage of your writing to help you determine what needs improving and/or correcting before writing the final version. Then give this checklist and your writing to a peer editor (a classmate) to use to edit your work.

Title of Writing Selection:_____

Things to Check	Writer's Checklist		Peer Editor's Checklist	
	Yes	No	Yes	No
1. Does the writing have a topic sentence and a concluding sentence?				
2. Does the writing explain how to do something in a logical order? Are any steps left out?				
3. Is the reader able to understand how to complete the task explained?				
4. Does the writing make sense and is it easy to read?				
5. Did the writer use details that help explain the steps?				
6. Did the writer use transitional words such as *first, next, then,* and *finally*?				
7. Does each sentence begin with a capital letter?				
8. Does each sentence have an ending punctuation mark?				
9. Did the writer use complete sentences?				
10. Did the writer check for misspelled words?				
11. Is each paragraph indented?				

☆ If the peer editor checked "No" in any box above, discuss it with the editor.

Think About It!

I think I did a _____ job on this writing selection because…

_____

_____

Expository-Writing Assessment

Student's Name: _____   **Date:** _____

Title of Writing: _____

Assessment Items	Agree	Disagree
1. The writing selection has a topic sentence and concluding sentence.		
2. The writing selection explains how to do something.		
3. The writing selection shows a logical order in the steps of the explanation.		
4. The writing selection makes sense; it is easy to read.		
5. Specific details are used to enhance the explained steps.		
6. All details relate to the topic.		
7. Descriptive words and details are used.		
8. Transitional words such as *first, next, then,* and *finally* are used.		
9. Correct punctuation and capitalization are used.		
10. Each word is spelled correctly.		
11. Run-on sentences and incomplete sentences are avoided.		
12. Each verb agrees with its subject.		
13. All proper nouns are capitalized.		
14. Each paragraph is indented.		
15. Apostrophes are correctly used to form contractions and to show possession.		

Comments: _____

_____

_____

_____

Editing Symbols

Writers use special marks called *editing symbols* to help them edit and revise their work. Editing symbols are used to show what changes a writer wants to make in his or her writing.

Symbol	Meaning	Example
⬯	Correct spelling.	⟨animl⟩
ℰ	Delete or remove.	dogg℮
◡	Close the gap.	f◡sh
∧	Add a letter or word.	lives in ∧tree ∧a
#	Make a space.	flies#south
∿	Reverse the order of a letter, a word, or words.	plants eats
∧⸴	Insert a comma.	the crab∧⸴ an arthropod∧⸴
⊙	Insert a period.	Cats purr⊙
⌄	Insert an apostrophe.	a deer⌄s antlers
⌄⌄ ⌄⌄	Insert quotation marks.	She said,⌄⌄Look at the pig.⌄⌄
≡	Make the letter a capital.	birds≡ eat seeds.
/	Make the letter lowercase.	a S̸nowshoe hare
¶	Start a new paragraph.	¶Some dogs have tails.